Playing With Love

Happy Accidents of a Young Pianist's Journey to a Triumph Over Cancer

By Mark Westcott

Playing With Love

Happy Accidents of a Young Pianist's Journey to a Triumph Over Cancer

By Mark Westcott

© 2014 Mark Westcott. All rights reserved.
ISBN: 978-1-312-02154-9

First Edition: March 2014

No part of this book may be reproduced or transmitted in any form or by any means, without express written permission from Mark Westcott. All rights for publishing this book or portions thereof in other languages are contracted by the author.

"The opposite of fear is not courage—it is love."

— a US Marine in Iraq —

A Special Kind of Lunatic

The gentlemen members of what we today call concert pianists generally appear in recital or in front of the members of a symphony orchestra in a traditional suit of evening clothes called tails. An elegant remnant of the era in which this hybrid soloist first emerged before the public, this wardrobe not only looks suitable before the commanding presence of a half ton of black piano but is also surprisingly comfortable in which to play. With the sides of a normal suit-type or tuxedo jacket cut away, the extra long panels of fabric, or tails, are draped behind, their weight holding the garment back and out of the way of busy arms. Furthermore, the sides of a normal jacket have a nasty habit of getting pinned down between the bench and the pianist's legs, constricting gradually tighter with any tiny movement of the torso until one would just as soon tear them off.

Beyond matters of tradition, a symbol of professional status, or the practical benefits of clever design, tails suggest the deliberate similarity of a uniform. Minimizing visual differences between artists, attention to the individuality of each is focused toward the sound of his playing alone. Just as the music of any great composer possesses an inimitable quality often recognizable in an instant, the great performers of their music are also set above the rest by a similar uniqueness: the musical signature of each. Revealed in this artistic identity is an entire life: a history, a journey—each moment becoming part of that signature.

As an aspiring high school pianist, I was assured that talent, zeal, and hard work could carry me far. During the first decade of the Cold War, I was awestruck by Van Cliburn's stunning victory in Moscow and the ticker-tape parade that followed in New York. When lanky, handsome

Van came through Portland, Oregon, I went alone to hear him play the Tchaikovsky Concerto. The whole affair seemed grand, but somehow out of reach. As I sat with chills and a pounding heart in the darkened hall, any suggestion of a connection to my daily practice in a middle-class Portland home seemed impossible.

Miraculously, years of hard work, great teaching, and happy accidents would later bring me to perform on many of the very same platforms Van himself played upon. In Chicago, Berlin, Sydney, and so many others I, too, would bring to some youngsters a little bit of what Van had brought to me.

My offering here is in small part about that miracle. Moreover it is about what most folks don't see out on stage in fine formal clothes—the inherent conflicts between a great artistic tradition and the chaotic ways of the world. And, it's about the special kind of lunatic, on fire and crazy in love enough to pursue one in the other. It's about growing up—despite valiant efforts not to do so.

The explanation behind why I set about to write all of this can perhaps begin by knowing that my own particular set of handcrafted tales were carefully stored in mothballs for a decade, where they remain.

In the early 90s what seemed an innocuous patch of dry skin on the bridge of my nose grew oddly persistent. Following its removal and a biopsy, I was given the ominous news that mixed in with a relatively harmless malignancy was a truly dangerous, virulent, and unpredictable type of cell. What followed was a ten-year battle during which I lost a substantial portion of my face not just once, but yet again in an even more destructive recurrence requiring numerous additional surgeries, as well as a full month of radiation therapy. To be sure, this last therapeutic hurdle did defeat my foe, but in return cost me a final price—all my teeth.

When the siege began, I returned to live in the safety of my family home in Portland, Oregon. My father had died just before, but my mother, turning eighty, was still bright and vigorous. In her care, and assisted by the nursing skills of my dog, Kypp, I recovered from two dozen surgeries. Upon each return from the hospital, I labored up the few stairs to the main floor directly to the living room couch. Each time after easing myself down and flicking on the TV in an effort to forget, Kypp silently hopped up and tiptoed between my legs, tenderly resting his head on my lap.

During those years, as much as I was forced to leave behind, my practice at the piano remained a daily indispensable. I practiced constantly, day and night—sometimes even all night, dragging merrily into the kitchen to see my mother making her morning coffee. I practiced in pajamas, in a bathrobe, in sweats, but most often in bandages—each time delivered from pain, from worry and from loss as long as I could work. Despite my ordeal, I was safe, I was home, I was loved, and I loved what I did more than ever. I had realized early on that I would have a lot more to say about the condition of my playing than the condition of my face.

The difficulty, dread, and real loss endured by any long-term patient can be enormous, sparing no facet of life. With complete candor I've said while smiling more than once, "I've lost more than most folks dream of having." Yet not only was my natural love of life intact, it seemed stronger than ever. Despite what I saw as I looked in the mirror, my sense of self-image and self-esteem had somehow not appreciably worsened. Before long I would even begin to develop an odd pride in my survival, regardless of the scars on my face, the likes of which once prompted a four-year-old in a nearby shopping mall to stop dead in his tracks and chirp, "Are you a burn victim?" When his mother began to admonish him in hushed tones, I had already knelt down with a smile to extend a handshake and introduce myself. I then reminded his mother that it seemed he'd been well taught not to judge unusual looking people poorly, but that perhaps his only misunderstanding was that a question such as his was not necessarily the best conversation opener.

One morning following my last surgery, my mother came into the living room with an odd look on her face. "Do you know, Mark, I just realized as I was thinking in the kitchen, that through this whole thing I have never heard you complain, not once."

I was stunned by her remark, but even more when I realized its truth. As I asked myself how this could have been, one reason behind writing this book presented itself with the answer: that during my young years in single-minded pursuit of an elusive goal—to play my best—I had learned at a fundamental level an important lesson or attitude toward life that now sustained me. It certainly was not an overabundance of courage—I'd been scared stiff most of the time. During the days just after a surgery I'd even managed to perform the vigil of wound care and changing bandages without looking directly into the mirror. I'd suffered plenty of both anger and grief over a long list of losses starting with my face, through most of my assets, to the career I'd chased after since a teenager.

It seemed to me that my feelings mirrored those of most other people in a similar position, with one surprising exception: as the battle ground on, surgery after surgery, and despite the medical prison that had become my day-to-day life, I became intoxicated with and susceptible to the surprising sweetness of the simple fact of life itself.

Not only had I converted the garage into a beautiful and comfortable studio, I'd found a plethora of pleasures, my indulgence in each being only now possible. I also remodeled the kitchen, finding stupendous appliances at great prices in the back rooms of area stores. I swam through my small collection of cookbooks to the delight of my mother, as well as friends who came by just to spend time together in a great kitchen concocting masterpieces of culinary indulgence.

I worked out constantly, returning to my college weight and looking physically even better—from the neck down. Often with a friend, and always in Kypp's charming company, I meandered through the Oregon wilderness, fishing and hiking—often sleeping in the middle of nowhere, comfortable and safe in my car. Remnants of a childhood curiosity and part of my abiding love of the natural world were resurrected with gardening, which culminated in show-quality chrysanthemums.

This mania for living was not just an effort in diversion from the unpleasant reality of my life, but a near insatiable appetite spurred on by what seemed the constant inner stirring of life itself—one which served to rescue me as the situation steadily worsened. During those moments in which I was compelled to pray, instead of pleas for relief or help of some kind, I prayed only to express my deep gratitude for continued survival. Most of this book was written during that long, difficult battle. Doing so has been part of my rescue.

My other motives in writing this book are simple: a gift, as it were, to the many people who have given me innumerable kindnesses along the way; and an effort to find some order in chaos—perhaps simply by accepting it. Any excursions into sharing life lessons from this unique journey are tempered by my belief that people can learn only what they are prepared to understand.

This is neither an autobiography nor an exposé. Perhaps once too often someone has said, "You know, Mark, you should write that down." During these reflections, an occasional unpleasant event may have been recalled. Should some people mentioned here seem a bit less magnificent than a publicist's portrayal, not they, but my expectations are at fault.

6   **Playing With Love**

Keys to the Kingdom

During my boyhood, post-war Portland produced truly outstanding young pianists. Soon he or she would be on the way to study at a fine school of music with a first-rate teacher and a full scholarship.

Despite the fact that by age twenty-three I would take prizes in several respectable international competitions, as a youngster growing up in Portland, Oregon, I was anything but a big fish in the proverbial small pond. And thank God, because I had to work like mad.

During the postwar years, Portland was blessed to have several unusually fine private teachers with impressive degrees from major conservatories and schools of music. Some were no less than living links to the great tradition, having studied with the descendents of Busoni and Leschetizky, legendary heirs to the father creator, Franz Liszt.

Before Liszt, there were no concert pianists as we use the term today. The keyboard was the basic tool of the composer. Along with their transcendent and all but forgotten skills as improvisers, for the most part composers were the sole performers of their own music. Playing the piano to a level of virtuosity was an important part of achieving the recognition needed to promote and secure performances of their compositions for orchestra, chamber music and other idioms.

Liszt's vision, charisma, and endless generosity made him the most famous personality for many years of his own lifetime throughout the artistic and intellectual world. Combined with his awesome gifts as a pianist, his particular niche in history created a lasting need for a new species of musical artist.

Liszt played everything by everyone in his recitals, not just his own works, but also the big Bach Partitas and the Goldberg Variations, works of Mozart and Haydn, and all the Beethoven Sonatas—all of them. His ability to sight-read was legendary. His grasp of musical styles and the sheer technical and tonal arsenal at his disposal, combined with a supreme knowledge of the composer's workshop—harmony, melodic structure, musical form—enabled him to perform by memory an enormous body of works. As Bach had unified the many styles of composition that went before him, Liszt did so pianistically, creating a revolution in performance, and thus paving the way for super-pianists like Busoni, Leschetitzky, Anton Rubenstein, Rachmaninoff, Hofmann, Gieseking, Cortot, and Solomon.

Liszt's alter ego was Chopin, who, due to the unquestioned genius of his compositions and playing, overcame a personal reclusiveness to share a large portion of credit for fathering the new breed of pianists. Unlike Liszt, Chopin centered his compositional genius almost exclusively to works written for the piano, one which is only recently and rightly being compared to the loftiest levels of Bach, Beethoven, Mozart, and Brahms. Also unlike Liszt, Chopin rarely played works of other or earlier composers.

Liszt was in many ways a larger figure. He not only had a voracious musical appetite, a wide-open love of life, and the daring soul of a romantic era hero, he was an endless, all but superhuman font of energy—a genuine dynamo. Judging by his vast compositional output, concert activities, and a personal life which in itself would dwarf those of any other ten men, it must have seemed to him that the rest of the world and the mere mortals in it existed in some kind of slow motion.

Who was in fact a greater composer or even a greater pianist is not a certainty, however. In the view of many, Chopin may have been better in both ways. But it took someone like Liszt to create the need, codify the training process, demonstrate the level of ability and captivate a fifty-year swatch of ardent romantic era audiences to give birth to the special organism we now call a concert pianist. Amidst the public spectacle which was Franz Liszt, his ceaseless re-working and performing of the works of both contemporaries and predecessors created the artistic inertia his students and others who followed would continue.

I should perhaps have started taking lessons at the age of five or six. But despite my conspicuous musical talent, evidenced by my love for music of all kinds, a good singing voice, a quick ear, and excellent coordination, my parents were skeptical about me starting piano lessons. They had not only been unable to connect with a teacher worthy of my eager abilities, but also one capable of dealing with the special problems of a little boy of exceedingly high spirits (or, as my mother used to say, "with ants in his pants"). Mom's excellent background as a singer and my dad's unique understanding of education made them alert to the importance of finding a teacher who would give me a good foundation. Again and again my mother told me that the time and the right person would come. I had to try to be patient in the meantime—not a virtue natural to my character.

When the search brought me to Aurora Underwood, the true extent of my parents' wisdom unfolded with beautiful symmetry. Raised in the arid and sparsely populated country of Eastern Washington, the young Aurora Potter had likewise benefited from the wisdom of parents able to see beyond their own histories to find a better way for their child. Aurora's diligence and fiery passion as a young adult took her to the highest echelons of musical study in this country and abroad. However, as she confided in my mother, it was her husband, Rex Underwood, an outstanding violinist and teacher, who brought her musical abilities to fruition.

With a start that may have been two or three crucial years late, I at least was fortunate not to suffer from bad habits or serious misunderstandings when I came under the care of the great Mrs. Underwood. Her only misgiving about the lively, rosy-cheeked blond boy for whom she created a space in her studio, was that from the perspective of her own background, my mother had waited a bit too long, and that even she might not be able to make up for the delay in early training. This would be the only thing about which my beloved Mrs. Underwood would be wrong—not due to my gifts but to her humble estimate of her own remarkable teaching abilities.

Weighing less than one hundred pounds, she was an awesome pianist with a big, bravura, brilliant approach. In every way, whether conveying musical theory, sight-reading, musicianship, organization of practice, or technique, forging a pianist's anatomy from young hands and arms, Mrs. Underwood's teaching was sure-footed, well-balanced wizardry.

I didn't even know the notes of the piano when we began in the fall just following my ninth birthday. But only three short years passed until I was set adrift to study and practice on my own for several weeks during a summer spent in lovely little Taft, on the Oregon coast. There I tackled the second and third movements of the Grieg Piano Concerto.

For a twelve-year-old boy with his own rowboat, fishing pole, crab trap, clam shovel, and "ants in his pants," the seduction of a million adventures from the summer's free roaming of the magical Oregon Coast scored the only time in memory during which my mother felt compelled to insist on an hour's daily practice. This summertime minimum would shortly be viewed as laughable, but along with the help of the local grade-school principal, who provided a key for a daily visit to a spinet piano in the deserted school, my mother's rare interference with my otherwise self-determined practice schedule wisely bridged a potentially costly lapse in my early training under Aurora. The challenge in teaching myself two movements of the Grieg Concerto would be of immeasurable value in solidifying all I'd learned to that point.

Children can be taught complex disciplines to amazing levels. But the nature of music itself demands subtleties which cannot be fully taught; mimicked, even amazingly well, but not fully learned. Only in the private endeavor between student and music can the special kind of personal relationship, which is at the very heart of true learning, be found. The teacher must provide the foundation of understanding and encourage the enthusiasm for its pursuit but carefully avoid stifling it with too much interference. It is a delicate and difficult balance for the teacher. Such unassisted study marks the beginning of genuine musical, as well as personal, maturity for a developing youngster.

After Labor Day I came to my first lesson and played through the second and third movements of the Grieg for Mrs. Underwood. I will never forget that moment in her large, elegant studio as we finished—she, of course, playing the orchestral part on a second Steinway grand. Shortly after, on a rainy weekend afternoon, I came upstairs from my practice on the Schumann Koncertstücke in G Major, Op. 92, to tell my horrified mother that I wanted to be a professional pianist.

Only a few years later, weekends, vacations, and eventually almost every Wednesday became the basis for continuing intensive practice. During these regular seclusions, I forged the habit, later described by a friend, of stalking the piano like a large predatory cat, circling a piece or the numerous problem passages of a large work with cool, determined confidence only to be found in an environment of uninterrupted and untroubled pursuit. Driven relentlessly by my love of music a bit beyond my immediate reach, I learned during the summer of my twelfth birthday to believe in the simple promise of good work, forging a future with my own hands.

Mrs. Underwood had taught me the best and rarest lesson of all: to teach myself. But my parents were the ones who provided the trust, personal freedom, and support to explore my love of music and play on my own terms. They demanded only that I do my very best.

If Mrs. Underwood was my primary piano teacher, my mother might very well have been my all-around musical mentor. A competent pianist, she was no less than a world-class dramatic soprano with serious and prolonged study in New York. The outbreak of World War II and her new husband's transfer out of New York City to officer's training school in the South combined, with the responsibilities of a new family, to derail a promising professional singing career.

If her knowledge of piano playing was inexact, her musical and performer's instincts were flawless. She sat with me from the very beginning, all the way through my high-school years, listening patiently and attentively to everything I played, demanding a singer's degree of dramatic and story-like intensity.

Occasionally when my work between lessons slacked off, during the ride home from Mrs. Underwood's studio she would calmly say to me, "Perhaps we should just put aside lessons for a little while until you're feeling more like working." That was usually all it took to have me working again at my full potential.

Later in my life, sometimes when I would play important recitals or concertos with major orchestras, it was my great pleasure to have her with me. At those times we shared not only the rewards of something we had worked toward in tandem, but also something that I often regretted had not been fulfilled in her own life.

Portland drew many top artists for recitals and concerto performances. As a teenager I managed to hear most of them, often alone. But the music room of the main library became the altar of my obsession. There, on countless afternoons, I sat transfixed with earphones and a score, listening to legendary artists, nearly all of whom had died long before my time. There I found the mother lode. I listened in awe, surprise and even shock to an earlier generation of artists whose playing brought the great tradition harkening back to Liszt to my young ears and heart with a fabulous richness, variety of colors, and deep personal persuasion.

Most of all, the sheer uniqueness of their individual playing captivated me. Often hearing poorly engineered or damaged recordings, I was still drawn toward playing I sensed to be very different from most living pianists. Schnabel, Cortot, Hofmann, Gieseking, Rachmaninoff and Solomon were among those who became my private mentors.

At fifteen I won the annual concerto competition of the famed Portland Junior Symphony and the opportunity to perform the Beethoven 3rd Concerto with them the next fall. That experience, with a difficult and mature work, created for me a new perception of the true size of my potential. From then on, my sights were on things other than the hometown squabbles and politics of local contests. Besides one or two library afternoons each week, listening to nearly everybody play everything, I continued choosing and working out some of my pieces all on my own. This was not a challenge to Mrs. Underwood's authority or wisdom but a testament to her genius, and she supported it.

When I heard Horowitz's recording of the Schumann Toccata, I nearly flipped. Now sixteen, somehow I had to play it. Mrs. Underwood shuddered when I brought it up at a lesson, but a week or two later, I spotted the score on the corner of her black Steinway. During a busy moment I snitched it, noticing that it already had my name on it, and tucked it into my music. That night, I dove into the labyrinth of problems with a foolhardy abandon. The next week I played it for Aurora. A week later I added it to the Papillons, Op. 2 of Schumann on a small program for a statewide music teacher's meeting. I was finding my courage and the special excitement that comes with big challenges.

Controversy swirls around the merits of competitions. Horowitz, who I don't believe ever entered a competition, felt that the problem with them was the manner in which they are generally judged. He felt, and I think rightly so, that far too often, good attributes like imagination, individuality, musical soundness, and projection are overlooked while too often bland playing with few objectionable or controversial traits prevails.

Often, following a big competition, stories of political intrigues or knockdown, drag out arguments in jury deliberations circulate in the student lounges of the big schools of music. When tossing one's hat into this particular ring, one has to have the proper attitude and be philosophically and emotionally prepared, not only to gain wisdom with a loss (no matter how unfair it may seem), but to see the good fortune of a victory in proper perspective as well.

At seventeen, just after graduation, I participated in the prestigious Young Musicians Foundation Debut Auditions in Los Angeles. One of my rivals in Portland had made a very good showing the year before, and Mrs. Underwood thought my time had come. Of the nearly one hundred pianists from all over the country, I was the second youngest. Nearly all were of college age or beyond—up to age twenty-five. Most of us were housed in the dormitories at UCLA. The very first person I met was Eugene Fodor, the wonderful violinist, who was a year younger than I. Eugene could play anything on the violin upside-down and backwards and was even a pretty good pianist as well. In the presence of his huge smile and equal energy, I found deliverance from the terror within me.

The competition itself was held in famous Royce Hall. When I played in the first round, all I remember is being scared stiff. My program included the Bach, Toccata in D Major, Beethoven's, Sonata Op. 10, No. 3, Brahms, 6 Piano Pieces Op. 118, Liszt, "La Campanella", Debussy, Suite "Pour le Piano", the Schumann Concerto and the Schumann Toccata thrown in—which I had been playing every chance I got for the whole year prior, and which had long since been nicknamed "Mark's Toccata" by my friends.

At the end of a long afternoon, I was stunned to be called back for another hearing. Suddenly I felt that there might be more in store for me than just the experience of hearing all the others. I was tired and hungry, but felt that if I could calm down and really play my best, something good might happen.

As before, I began with one of the Brahms; I had played the first two in the morning, but it would now be the more elusive 4th, not the kind of thing one expects from a kid. Having chosen and studied all six myself as a labor of love, I hoped it could help to separate me from the others. Sure enough, when I finished the judges were smiling broadly. I felt that here for these judges, big-time professionals, my boyish looks were not obscuring the qualities that sometimes went over the heads of the judges back at home. Then a surprise—they wanted to hear the treacherous Toccata again!

It had been OK in the morning, but not my best—nervous and probably a bit messy now and then. Now I was in this thing up to my neck and being tested. Nevertheless, unlike many previous contest experiences in Portland, I sensed that I was being sized up strictly on my playing. Nervous shakes were gone, replaced by clear wit and all the buoyant strength I needed.

When it was over, I was thanked and asked to wait with the others. Two or three played; then all the participants were called out for the results. The finals in piano would be the night after next and would include the wife of the first cellist of the Boston Symphony, then twenty-five-year-old Virginia Eskin, and—guess who? Me.

Virginia was formidable. With Ravel's "Gaspard de la Nuit" and the Brahms 1st Concerto, her program was packed with big, mature, complex works suitable for the seasoned player she was. But I had to be there for a reason. Somehow my playing had made me prevail over a hundred college and grad-school pianists from around the country. The only way I'd have a chance of surviving the pressure of over two dozen jurors whose names read like a Who's Who in music, and an audience of 3,000, would be to practice like mad the next day and escape to a movie the next night to take my mind off the relentless pressure.

In the moments before I played, I experienced a kind of aloneness which over the years would become a frequent companion; a state that could bring me to my very best or, in the onset of a poor attitude, turn on me with a vengeance. It's a moment of truth that can make or break a really tough situation, one in which you will either fall far short of your standards or sail to a realm actually beyond your abilities. In that moment, the simple reason behind why you play can matter most of all. I suppose some people would have prayed, but the torture of my own trivial fears has never seemed worthy of prayer.

As Virginia left the stage to thunderous applause, I stood in the darkened backstage—head down, hands folded and motionless. I had no idea what to do and barely knew where I was and what I was doing. I only knew that I was terrified and felt terribly alone. Just then, a woman on the board of the foundation who was helping backstage touched me on the shoulder and asked me how I was feeling. She'd seen exactly the state I was in and left her post at the entrance to the platform to talk to me. All of her maternal instincts must have been at work, because just the simple act of her coming over to chat helped me to escape from the torment of my isolation.

"I've never been so scared in my whole life," I said shakily. Without a moment's pause, she hugged me tenderly and then drew away to look firmly into my eyes. "Of course you are," she said. "I'm scared, and I'm not even playing!"

We both laughed nervously. Then she took me by the hands and said, "You surprised everyone so completely that they had to hear you again just to believe their ears. You look like such a boy, but playing Brahms with such warmth and maturity, and that Toccata—my God!"

She pulled me closer, now whispering intensely, "Now listen, sweetheart, what would your mother tell you right now if she were here?"

I knew the answer in mid-question. "To just play my best. She'd say that's all I can do."

"Good advice. Your mother knows, doesn't she? She knows you are ready. And you are playing here, now, because you're ready."

I smiled with a mix of relief and embarrassment as mortal terror and confusion were gradually replaced by excitement and a feeling of pride. Here I was, finally heard by a jury of professionals, and it was time to confirm the honor bestowed by this opportunity. Playing less than my best was out of the question.

As I stepped onto the platform and walked that very long walk to the piano at center stage of a very large hall, I was no longer alone. With me were all of the artists and composers I'd encountered at my lessons and during all those long, magnificent afternoons at the library. Aurora had given me the keys to the kingdom. I walked before that audience as a proud member of a great tradition, a legacy which I had not only touched, but of which I might someday be a part.

In a sense, I would not be judged by the jury so much as by all those artists and composers I'd troubled to explore, to question and to admire. The outcome was somehow becoming unimportant, for at that moment I realized how rich my life truly was and that I had already discovered what Aurora had sent me to Los Angeles to learn.

Young as I was, I was no longer a boy from Portland. I was taking my first steps as a young artist. Not because I had in any way arrived, but thanks to Aurora's wonderful teaching I was beginning to think and behave like a living link to the great tradition and pianists of the past.

———◆———

Four years later, on the weekend following my third prize in the Van Cliburn Competition, I found myself in Boston visiting Michael Tilson-Thomas, the new assistant conductor to the Boston Symphony Orchestra. The first evening, we sat in the video booth at Symphony Hall to see Guilini guest conduct. Just following, I ran smack into Virginia Eskin backstage. I introduced myself and cautiously queried her about remembering me from L.A. and the Young Musicians Foundation some years back—assuming she knew that the brat who'd beaten her then had just taken third prize in the Cliburn.

With a faraway look in her eye, as if recalling a really bad restaurant, she said, "Oh yes. Are you still playing?"

Touché.

A few years ago, I saw Virginia for the first time in many, again in Boston, still beautiful and playing up a storm. I reminded her of that meeting backstage and how she had waited for years to nail me for beating her. We both laughed until we were nearly sick.

———◆———

Years later, inheriting the music library of my beloved teacher was a humbling experience as I began to grasp the scope of her awesome repertoire. Nearly every work of Chopin was heavily marked from study, as were tons of Liszt, more than half of the Beethoven Sonatas, all of the big Schumann works, most of the Brahms, and literally hundreds of lesser known short works.

Mrs. Underwood's prowess as a chamber and duo player was no less impressive. The wonderful violinist Zvi Zeitland told me a story about meeting her many years back during his first tour of the West Coast. He was engaged to play an all-Beethoven Sonata program at the University of Oregon in Eugene where Dr. and Mrs. Underwood headed up what was at that time an extension of the Juilliard School. A terrible blizzard stalled his travel and blocked all communication, leaving more than a little confusion about which of the ten sonatas for piano and violin were programmed. When Zvi arrived, he was stunned to discover at first rehearsal that the diminutive Aurora Underwood had prepared them all. Just in case.

A careful search in the fall of 1970 led me to a brilliant young pianist and teacher at The Oberlin Conservatory of Music named John Perry. I was blessed to be in the tutelage of a world-class musician already at the very top of his form and at a school with magnificent facilities. I worked like a slave.

Many future summers would become pilgrimages to study with one of the most mysterious personalities I have known, Frank Mannheimer, who, along with Cécile Genhart at Eastman, formed the two principal artistic influences of Mr. Perry's own study as a young man. The gifts of these three later teachers would come to rest atop the foundation Mrs. Underwood's genius had provided to form a healthy and independent musical personality that would carry me toward my own artistic future.

During one of my early lessons with the legendary Mrs. Genhart at Eastman, she stopped me after the sprawling and complex slow movement of Beethoven's "Hammerklavier" Sonata. After a moment's reflection she said, "Who was your teacher?" I thought she knew, and I politely reminded her of my four years at Oberlin with her former student, John Perry.

"No," she said, "not Perry. Who was your *teacher*?"

"Well, as you know, I've worked in the summers with Mr. Mannheimer..."

But again, she broke me off asking, "Who was your *teacher*?"

"Well, my first teacher, who I worked with for nine years, was Aurora Underwood in Portland, where I was raised."

"Yes," *she* sighed, "she is responsible. I must meet her."

And although they did not meet, a week later Mrs. Underwood received a letter from Mrs. Genhart that she cherished for the rest of her life.

When I was in my early thirties, I was honored to be the featured artist at the National Convention for the Music Teachers National Association (MTNA). After the recital's intermission, I had the pleasure of telling the audience filled with private teachers from around the country that story. Mrs. Underwood was in the audience.

Good Times in Texas

When I was a sophomore at Oberlin, I came to Houston to compete in a competition run by the Symphony. I was put up at the home of a Mr. and Mrs. Johnson, in the spiffiest neighborhood in town. They were lovely but mysterious people—gracious, with a sturdy warmth. Mrs. Johnson was whimsical and good natured. She loved and wrote poetry but was also fully capable on the ranch they owned in the hill country just outside Austin. Mr. Johnson was a Trumanesque democrat and the recently retired vice president of a major corporation. His true love was the ranch and the connection it provided to the natural world. Like several men I have known and liked, I shared this spiritual connection with him.

In those days, I often had problems sleeping the night before a performance, especially if I would have to play in the morning. At the Johnson home in Houston, I spent a miserable night during which I didn't sleep at all. The next day I did not play well and was informed that I was not to be called back. With a weekend left before returning to school, the Johnsons took me to their ranch, next door to President Johnson's ranch—a fact revealed by a helicopter with the Presidential Seal passing just overhead.

The Johnsons were more interested in my promise than my failure. They had made some calls and spoken with some folks who had heard me when I had won the competition in L.A. On Sunday afternoon as we sat on the porch sipping mint juleps, Mr. Johnson said that they would like to provide the remaining expenses for my studies at Oberlin and graduate school, summers and other outside study, as well as helping with a first European tour. I was stunned. Returning to school, I had a sense of tremendous responsibility. Someone had put money down on me. I wasn't going to disappoint them.

My relationship with the Johnsons would provide for my future study, a cherished friendship, and the basis of many adventures. Before long it was understood that I would visit them on their ranch every chance I could. As working cattle ranches go, this 5,000 acre ranch was only a toy. Of several homes on the bluff overlooking the Lady Halifax River, the oldest was a real work of art from an era of very special country houses built throughout Texas. Great chunks of colorful sandstone were neatly fitted and mortared, with cedar beams supporting the roof and around the doors and windows. The aroma of stone and cedar, used to repel bugs and scorpions, still lingered pungently after many years.

I found this time delightful in the presence of people interested in my pianistic skills who made no fuss about my hands. There was, however, a certain irony that while betting a considerable amount of money and support on a concert pianist, they sometimes provided situations of inherent recklessness or even danger.

I learned to ride and care for my own horse and worked with ranch hands mending fences. In order to spare my hind-end the pain of daily rides after long breaks at school, a horse with an especially gentle walk was provided. However, the reason no one else rode him became apparent the first—and last—time I pulled him up to a sudden stop. When he stiffened up his forelegs and slammed to a stop on his front feet, I was catapulted straight up into an overhanging oak tree and nearly knocked out cold.

Mr. Johnson, who had a wicked sense of humor, once asked me if I'd like to go swimming. Although I'm almost a competition level swimmer, I'm a little timid about swimming in rivers or lakes, unless I know the inhabitants or the water is clear. He assured me that the stretch in front of the house, from a small dock up a couple of hundred yards to a large rock in mid-river, was perfectly safe. I had no reason not to believe him. I think I might have been a bit too ready to show off my good crawl, and in an effort to survive the Texas heat, I found some shorts and went down to the river. At the dock, I was joined by J.M. and a couple of others who seemed oddly eager to see how well I could swim. He dared me to beat the record from the dock to the rock and back again.

On the spot, J. M. put forward a plausible number and suggested that if I would give it a shot, I might be the new record holder. As he consulted his watch I heard the words, "Ready, set, go," dove into the water, and swam for all I was worth. About the time I expected to meet up with the rock and do one of my fancy flip turns, leftover from my swim team days as a kid, I found myself face to face with the most gigantic catfish in all creation. The apparition was so sudden and gruesome looking that I flew straight up out of the water with a terrible scream. I then proceeded to set the record for the frantic sprint back. Evidently, that monster was estimated to be well over a hundred pounds. This was one of J. M.'s two favorite pranks to play on unsuspecting guests.

The other was perhaps a little more spectacular. On my next trip to the ranch, at feeding time a number of us were standing next to the goat pen's eight-foot log fence. While we chatted with drinks in our hands, J. M. benignly handed me a very large bucket of goat feed and opened the door to the pen, which housed at least fifty goats ranging in size from a Chihuahua to a llama—a very large llama. I took no notice, for all the goats were milling around at the far end of the pen many yards away, and I assumed I was simply doing someone a favor to bring this bucket of feed to the trough in the middle. The gate was opened as I merrily walked forward.

Suddenly all fifty goats took notice of me coming with their dinner, and I became the target of a stampede. Dropping the bucket abruptly, I turned and scrambled the distance of the pen and actually jumped the high fence. Coming to my senses, I turned around to see the goats happily consuming their feed while the onlookers were gripped with uncontrollable laughter. I'm sure this scenario never failed to delight, but I'm just glad I'm here to tell the story. Heart attacks have happened with less fright.

During a later visit, I was joined by a lady friend from Austin for a day at the ranch. She was a fearless swimmer; previously having been caught in her car in one of Austin's flash floods, she had distinguished herself by swimming gamely through the torrents of raging water to safety. So, it was without hesitation that we went down to the dock and placed a simple aluminum canoe in the water for an afternoon ride.

Wearing just our swimsuits, we had considered one peril of which to be wary. Upstream from the Johnson's ranch house was an area of river considered the most heavily populated area of water moccasins anywhere in the country. A team of herpetological specialists came annually to collect specimens. Water moccasins can be quite large and are always scary looking, possessing highly aggressive personalities and a bite more lethal and lingering than that of a rattlesnake. In fact, a neighbor lady who had been bitten in the ankle years before still suffered terrible swelling and pain.

Only after Kathy and I thought we had absolute control over our vessel did we get the courage to carefully row upstream to the wide part of the river shaded by overhanging trees—and the home of at least hundreds of water moccasins that we could see at river's edge. Finally the time came to turn the canoe around and leave the devil's domain for the safety downstream where we might take a swim. Just at that moment Kathy said, "Mark, no matter what, do not move a muscle! Now very carefully, look down at your feet." As I gathered the courage, summoning the control to follow her instructions, there, between my feet was the biggest, hairiest, most demonic looking muscular beast of a spider I have ever seen. As it flexed its body up and down only inches from my bare feet, I was overwhelmed by a surge of adrenaline that betrayed all restraint, and I found myself doing a tarantella in a canoe violently listing in water moccasin infested waters. While Kathy gamely tried to steady our craft, I was swiping with my paddle for all I was worth at the monster between my feet. Finally, with a lucky shot or two, a leg flew off here or there until the beast lay in pieces.

When we returned to the ranch house, we brought up one of the thorny, three-inch long legs and were promptly given a book on local spiders. To our horror, we had been keeping company with a wolf spider. Preying on small birds and insects hardly my size, it is not exactly what one should see next to bare feet in a canoe listing about in the water moccasin capital of the world.

At the same time, during the late 60s, a menacing shadow over my otherwise single-minded pursuits at Oberlin was the Vietnam War and the draft. I had been lucky, but remained vulnerable for drafting, and President Johnson was doing a lot of it. When the new lottery system came during my junior year at Oberlin, I drew a high number and with it, a deep sigh of relief.

Just before returning to school for my senior year, I was on a summer campout at the Oregon Coast with some other young men in the same position. On a lovely evening we sat together in the moonlight around a huge blaze. Before long several took off in different directions on little walks as I was left alone at the fire. When a few guys camping down the beach came by, one stayed and settled by the fire with me.

He was typical of so many boys raised under the cuddly blanket of the American middle class, suddenly feeling adrift on an iceberg of fate. I'll never forget it. He was tall and strong, clear-eyed and rosy-cheeked in the heat of the fire. He told me that he'd just been through basic training at Fort Lewis, thought it had been "all right," but now he was off to Vietnam. At this point, his agitation became more apparent. He began to relate horror stories he had heard while going through basic training. One brutal statistic about life and death followed another: how long a guy in the jungle can escape injury, how many infantrymen are killed by booby traps, that kind of thing.

I asked what he would do. He replied that he would work on a rescue helicopter. There was a long pause. His chin lowered slowly down as he said softly, "I heard that the average life expectancy of a helicopter man under fire is about seven seconds." And he began to cry, as if he'd kept this rumored statistic more or less to himself until then. He leaned against me and sobbed. A long time passed while he cried in my arms in front of that bonfire. When he stopped, he looked away and said what sounded like "good night," but felt like "good bye." He dragged himself up slowly and disappeared like a ghost from the fire's orange glow into the darkness of his last summer night at home.

In the fall, with the image of that young soldier persisting in my memory, I returned to Oberlin for my senior year. Also, that same fall a visit to Texas would be of special importance: my participation in one of the world's biggest piano competitions: The Van Cliburn International Piano Competition in Fort Worth.

The word 'Texas' comes from the word tejas (Tehas) meaning friendly—an identity for Texans. During the Cliburn competition the hospitality was wrought with a downright vengeance—in fact it may be the only competition during which I actually gained weight. All I wanted to do, however, was practice. The huge preliminary program would be a big hurdle for us all. It was generally believed that someone other than Van himself dominated the creation of the sprawling repertoire requirements, Van would never have confused quantity for quality.

I would play Bach's "Italian Concerto," a Scarlatti Sonata, Beethoven's "Appassionata" Sonata, a Chopin Nocturne, a Brahms Intermezzo, two Transcendental Etudes ("Feux Follets" and "Harmonies de Soir") by Liszt, a Chopin Etude, the Mozart a-minor Sonata, Schumann's Symphonic Etudes, Ravel's "Scarbo", and perhaps more I've since forgotten. With a first stage like this, the big cut was made before Ft. Worth by all the people who just couldn't get it all ready. In the semifinals, there was another program not quite as demanding, but with a chamber work added. For the finals, four concerti were demanded. I prepared Brahms I, Beethoven IV, Barber, and the Rachmaninoff-Paganini Variations.

Just before the preliminaries began, all the contestants had to play fifteen minutes in the lobby of a sponsoring bank. We all sheepishly went downtown and had a laugh about doing our worst playing of the week, although some of us may have done our best. It was just after my offering that I met Glynn Baker. He was with one of his numerous buxom girlfriends. Glynn was very handsome, about six-foot-three and 200 pounds of a real merry Texan, with a delightful twinkle in his eyes and a genuine warmth, all mixed with an imposing intelligence that inspired quick affection from most and respect from all.

When he and his girlfriend heard the preliminaries, they bet on me to win. Fortunately, he made better bets in the commodities market—hand over fist. Determined to see his horse win the derby, Glynn took me under his wing and offered the chance to relax and escape from the pressures of the contest. I really didn't have much chance to even think it over. An offer from Glynn was an order you felt good about following. He had decided the matter. Indeed, it would prove a lucky thing to be befriended by this fellow.

Glynn was the kind of man one might expect to find in one of those little romance novels, almost too good to be real. With movie star looks and the body of a pro-athlete, he was thoroughly read and world traveled. In his late twenties he was ordained as a Buddhist Monk, later replacing such sacrifice and introspection with an easy acceptance of life without the least bit of pretension or assumption to 'know,' unlike some trendy pseudo-theologies of the time like EST or Scientology. I think he was still very much in touch with the boy inside, possessing a rare, easy charm, with an underlying danger.

Every day I looked forward to a little adventure with Glynn. When he'd pick me up, all I could think about were my pieces and what still needed work. Within minutes I was engrossed in the mysterious and beautiful stories he told, or giddy with some 'trouble' we might enjoy. His escapades with women put me into hysterics. He was probably a bit of a chauvinist, but women were nuts about him anyway.

Early one evening, two days before the semifinals, we went to a party hosted by Van Cliburn himself. It was a nice chance to speak with Van, who insisted on being called by his first name alone. In general, I'm not comfortable at parties and wasn't disappointed when Glynn asked to return to town to listen to me play my pieces for the next stage. Just after dark we arrived at the home where I practiced, and we closed ourselves off in the living room. I finished by playing the greatest and most mysterious of all Schubert's works, the Sonata in B-flat Major, Opus Posthumous. This work is truly the gospel according to Schubert. Playing it to just one person can be a test of the genuineness and honesty of a relationship. But after our time together, and due to Glynn himself, I found a special ease. When I finished, Glynn set aside his customary shy humor and leaped to his feet to embrace me. Fearing for my ribs, all I could do was stammer shyly, "I know. It's amazing." Both of us sat together, speaking in hushed excitement, sharing our collective awe of Schubert's masterpiece.

Glynn persisted in asking what, if anything, it was all about. I admitted to wondering whether it, like so much music, was really about anything in particular, but confessed I couldn't help my own ideas from taking hold. With that, he demanded I reveal some of them.

I began, "Well, Glynn, it's like: in the world, among all the struggle and the chaos, there is just a song..." I talked almost unconsciously, looking out of focus at the piano as if for guidance, sometimes playing a bit here or there. At one point Glynn said, "Mark, I'm so close to feeling what you mean, what you feel, but the words don't quite do it." He thrust one hand toward me in an unconscious gesture saying, "You know, I wish I could just plug in!"

Suddenly there was a deafening crack of sound as the small coffee table beside us flipped in mid air, turned completely upside down, and wobbled to a stop. The ashtray and tile coaster that had been on top now were under the overturned table which rested, neatly balanced. We sat aghast, looking at one another in a mixture of feelings, each waiting for the other person to break the silence. Finally, I asked, "What does this mean? Was this us? Or Schubert? Or what?" We both smiled in a bit of disbelief and some embarrassment over the inadequacy of words. There was no answer. Who could know? The important thing was that it was real, and suggested that the power of music is in the moment and much more than the realm of the beautiful.

Two days later I played the Mendelssohn D minor Trio, the commissioned work by Norman Dello Joio, and the Schubert and Bartok Piano Sonatas. I played my best. If I had played the first stage as well, I might have won first instead of third place. But my playing in competitions could be a bit uncertain. There was just something about the cool scrutiny of a contest which could throw me. In those days I was just too nervous to be as consistent as I should have been.¬¬

During my Oberlin years I studied with Frank Mannheimer each summer in Duluth, Minnesota. Mr. Mannheimer spent his winters in Santa Rosa, California, when he wasn't travelling in order to teach throughout the United States and Europe. Just before my fall participation in the Cliburn contest, he had seen to it that I was engaged by Santa Rosa's orchestra to play the Brahms Second Concerto.

In the spring of 1970 as those performances approached, I was twenty-one years old, just finishing my senior year, and stupidly fearless in the face of the challenge of the "Brahms 2nd." Due to the fall's good showing in the Cliburn, my year had been a steady series of away-from-school recitals. In May, the Brahms was not even memorized as I suddenly realized that I had only two weeks until the first rehearsal in Santa Rosa.

I was petrified. I was about to humiliate myself, and worse, Mr. Mannheimer.

I stayed on a rigid schedule of three two-hour sessions per day. I took out the super-hard passages and worked on them separately so as not to slow down the general progress. Sections that were repeated in another key I learned together. I worked quickly but as carefully and imaginatively as I could and did not waste energy worrying about the limits of time. I worked like a slave, but I got it, and well.

Only days before my flight to California, the horror of the Kent State massacre occurred. The next day an indescribable pall fell over the school. Everything ground to a halt—no classes, and everything locked. I was thrown out of the conservatory and ended up practicing my last days at the dean's house. Along with the rest of the country I viewed with apprehension the lack of restraint, the personal tragedies and the huge political about-face taking place, trying desperately to stay focused on my responsibilities.

I flew to California on schedule, and my performances received the first standing ovations in little Santa Rosa in many years. When three guys I'd grown up with drove in from Portland and L.A. to hear my first performance, I invited them to the reception thrown by a recently retired army officer and his wife. We were all draftable and opinionated, but agreed not to discuss the war. Generally, it was an easy promise to keep.

Since the mean age of the audience must have been 103, and all four of us were blond and about the same size, we collectively received glowing compliments from many of the guests. We each took turns making the appropriate gracious responses, and even went so far as to offer detailed discussions of the work. Finally, though, the old soldier who threw the party appeared in front of us, dressed in full uniform. After congratulating Don Robertson for his splendid performance, he stepped back to address our group.

"Well now, which one of you has served in our armed forces?" An awkward silence followed. "I know, I know what you're all thinking," he continued. And one by one he asked what our plans were for the military. Each of us courteously niggled out of an answer when finally he puffed up and declared, "Boys, it's a tough time and I know what you're all thinking. Sure it's a lousy war, but it's the only damned war we've got!" Some of us laughed, others cringed. I remembered the young soldier at the bonfire and felt lucky to be alive and with friends.

 As a talented young person in love with the magic of music develops, a level of listening and critical understanding of playing and music in general becomes almost painfully acute. As abilities progress upwards, so too the demands of the music itself seem always to outdistance even the greatest triumph. Thus, the very kind of artistic discernment necessary to bring the growth process along can itself fully undermine, if not discourage, the aspirant. Progressing from student to artist depends on mustering and sustaining a special kind of courage. Only when one understands that perfection does not exist for the musician, and accepts the rigors of constant growth and endless maintenance can peace of mind be found.

 All young people deal with issues of courage as they grow up, but for the young person on fire with an artistic pursuit, the issue of personal courage becomes the key to any chance of success. The young artist must find the courage to place the welfare of something else before his own natural need of easy acclaim or quick glory—to find the courage and take the daily leap of faith needed to face the near endless labor.

 There are stories about Horowitz and Serkin who, at the top of their form, were so artistically self-critical that they almost had to be coerced onto the stage. The ear of a musician can become that acute—so acute that even at the very height of their abilities such masters are all but daunted by their self-imposed demands. Imagine in a young artist, for whom fame and recognition has yet to occur, the difficulty in reckoning with the constant demand of this kind of unappeasable scrutiny. However, courage itself is not forged at the piano; its lessons come from life. What we bring to our playing and to the pursuit of something we love is a product of the joyful and courageous life we live not only as individuals, but also with those whom we love. My friend Don Robertson brought to me an unlikely but magnificent lesson in personal courage.

Attending Oberlin brought me relatively close to New York City—at least compared with Portland, Oregon. Although managing the hour by car to the Cleveland airport from a campus generally not allowing students to own cars proved more difficult than the short plane ride to New York City, before long I began a succession of trips, the accumulated effect of which would change me in many ways. During the summers of these same years, my return to the family home and the idyllic Oregon wilderness served to maintain a close connection with a few high-school friends, one of whom was Don. Don's family had a rustic cabin at the edge of the Metolius River located on the eastern side of the Cascade Mountains.

Don was an accomplished pianist and a good singer as well, participating during his college years in one of this country's foremost choral ensembles: the Occidental Glee Club. With Don's fervent love of and ongoing participation in music, and as the level of my professional activities as a pianist began to develop, it seemed a natural step that he might occasionally travel in the role of my one-man groupie, someone with whom to occasionally share high points of my endeavors. Despite Don's robust stature of 6'3", by nature he was exceedingly genteel and polite in any and all circumstances. It is possible that without the shared interests of my musical exploits our friendship may not have gone on as strongly as it did. But we chose to overlook any occasional differences in happy and mutual pursuit of a common interest.

Only a year after Don's attendance of my first performance of the Brahms 2nd in Santa Rosa, he called me at Eastman about the idea of traveling to Rochester with my mother in the spring to attend my Master's Degree recital. This would also provide the opportunity of meeting Cécile Genhart, as well as accompanying me and my mother to New York City over spring vacation the following week. This would be his first time to New York, and for my mother, the first return visit in the quarter-century since her marriage there to my father in the mid forties.

As luck would have it, just after their arrival in Rochester, most all of the airlines went on strike. Rather than sabotaging the New York City trip, we decided to make a four-hour journey by train. We arrived at Grand Central Station and, bags in hand, began the long walk toward the street, chattering excitedly all the way. Suddenly Don and I noticed that my mother was not only well ahead, but out of the doors on the sidewalk and running at nearly full clip. I left my bag with Don and headed off in pursuit. When I caught up with her she breathlessly told me that a young man had grabbed her suitcase, muttering something about carrying it for her to a nearby taxi. When we rounded the corner of a very large block, the man stopped, putting down the suitcase next to a lonely cab waiting at the side of the station. As we approached, every instinct in me raging, all I wanted to do was to get our belongings and all of us into the cab and safely away from the secluded area. As Don pulled up from behind, lugging the remaining bags, I hurriedly put everybody and the bags in the back seat of the cab.

    I pulled a five from my wallet for the man's dubious efforts in the hope of avoiding any trouble. He then demanded thirty-five dollars, citing that there had been six bags in all and that he expected to be paid five dollars per bag. Our real difficulties began when I informed him that he could neither count nor multiply, and that under the circumstances the five dollars was all but a gift, which he would be well advised to take. His reply was to pull a knife on me.

    With no time to be afraid nor to plan a strategy, old habits from my bit of high-school wrestling and the years on the living-room floor with my father took over. I dropped to the ground, yanking his feet out from beneath him, and as he fell, pulled him down by the arm, smashing his hand with the knife into the pavement. As the knife flew out of view, for the next long minute the fellow had his hands full with an irate 150-pound piano player. In desperation he scrambled to his feet and ran away.

    As I got up, dusted myself off, and noticed that I was in reasonably good condition under the circumstances, I also noticed that my mother, who had been trapped between the luggage on one side and Don on the other, was still in the process of trying to clamber over him to my assistance. I assured her that I was OK and got into the front seat of the cab. Still pumped full of adrenaline, and more than a bit shaken from the whole affair, I realized that during the entire operation Don had been sitting like a statue while I was being attacked at knifepoint just outside the cab. I went ballistic. I began by peppering the cab driver with questions about his possible affiliation with the bag grabber. Only his sheepish denials and quiet nodding spared him a good thrashing. I was mad as hell.

Poor Don got the tongue-lashing of his life for several blocks as we proceeded toward our hotel. Somewhere between 6th and 7th Avenues I realized that since everybody was OK, it would do no good to further jeopardize our long-anticipated arrival to New York by an ongoing harangue. In fact we not only had a lovely time, but the incident was never revisited—that is, until the next summer's reunion at the Metolius.

Following three hours of non-stop chattering en route to our annual summer reunion, upon our arrival we all hurriedly began to unpack, hoping for time in the late afternoon for a swim or perhaps some fly-fishing. During the blur of this activity Don quietly summoned me for a chat. A hundred yards upstream we perched on the railing of a small bridge—the traditional place for private exchanges. After reminding me of the New York incident, Don told me that although he'd had a fine time for the remainder of our trip, and that he wouldn't have been disappointed never to think of the incident again, as his voice began to change in timbre, he confessed that it haunted him ceaselessly.

"Mark, I've had to face dead on whether or not I was a coward, and whether or not my inaction could have caused you serious injury—or worse."

As I tried to break in, Don forcefully held up a hand, "Mark, don't say anything. I've really gotta get this off my chest. I know that you've probably never thought of it again. We've never talked about it—and for that I'm really grateful. This isn't about the tongue-lashing that I got—I had it coming. Look at what you'd just been through—I didn't do a thing. But if I had just so much as gotten out of the car, just having me stand there would have probably put a stop to it. And that's what haunts me day and night. What in the hell was I thinking of? Why didn't I do anything? For months since I've been in agony thinking of myself as a coward."

At this point I again tried to insert myself into the conversation, but Don would have none of it. "I'm not saying I wasn't scared. I was terrified. I think we were all terrified, even you—you even admitted so while you were chewing me out across town. That's what makes me so damned mad. You were terrified, but look what you did."

That's when I broke in. "Don, I didn't have a choice, and for the record I've never held this against you. You've got to remember I was absolutely crazy with adrenaline. I had just wrestled this guy to the street, and when I got into the cab that's when my fear really hit me. Of course I would've rather seen you jump out of the cab to help me; but Don, a situation like this was about as far from your personal experience as I could imagine."

Now Don interrupted, "Mark, I really don't think that I'm a coward. At least I don't want to think that. That's for damned sure. But I just wasn't raised with any of the rough and tumble you were exposed to that might have prepared me in some way for this kind of thing. Nevertheless, there was so much at stake, and it all happened so fast that despite my attempts to rationalize my behavior, or maybe lack of behavior, I've been stuck for these last months with this horrible shadow." And he began to cry.

I reached with one arm over the shoulders of my sobbing friend, pulling him toward me. "You just didn't know what to do. You've never been in a situation like that. You simply froze. I don't think you're a coward, Don. And despite my anger and fear at the time, I didn't think that you were a coward then, either. I just couldn't understand…"

"No, Mark. I mean I'm glad to hear you say that, and in a way I always knew you would, but it's not really how you feel that's important here. What I've been suffering under is the way I feel, and no amount of reflection and rationalization seems to be helping me out of my dilemma. And for a long time I have been truly suffering over this.

"The only thing that I've been able to come up with, the only thing that's done any good at all, is that I've needed to come here, just the two of us, and tell you about this—that maybe it will help. And to tell you, whatever the reasons behind what happened, to promise to you and to myself, I suppose, that if anything ever happens in my life like that again, I *will* act—I *will* do something, Mark. I've promised myself that, and I've wanted to come here today, to this spot, in this beautiful place, at this wonderful time—one which I hope we will share many times again, to tell you and promise to myself, I *will* act."

After a deep sigh he continued, "You know, just being able to tell you this, telling you about my decision to act, and that I know I will. I'll do my part."

"Don, that's because you already have acted—not just by telling me about this. I'm unimportant. What is important is the courage you've had to face this thing as magnificently as you have. From my point of view, my friend, you've got nothing to worry about."

———•———

Just after my graduate studies at Eastman were completed, before I would move to New York and tangle with the music business, and even before my first tour of debut concerts in Europe, I landed a big tour of British Columbia sponsored by the Canadian government. Although it would prove as demanding as nearly any other long tour I would later do, I was not only paid comparative peanuts, but lived and traveled far from the acceptable level of comfort and ease with which I would later become accustomed.

About two dozen recital performances would take place within less than six weeks' time on a tour roughly divided into two halves. For the first half, alone in a clunky station wagon, from town to town through lower British Columbia, I drove long days with just enough time to drop my things in a shabby motel, and hurry to the local high school auditorium for a quick warm up before my show.

Although the concerts were hugely attended and well received in small towns starved for any kind of visiting attraction, after two and a half weeks of this I was nearly exhausted, not to mention being darned sick and tired of my own company. My ongoing efforts for relief from this lonely ordeal were consistently thwarted by the only radio stations which I was able to pull in on my scratchy car radio, being all but saturated with that year's hit song, Gilbert O. Sullivan's, "Alone Again, Naturally". This little ballad's painful reminder of my general state was drilled into my head so relentlessly that I can still sing it with all the lyrics to this day.

As an intended reprieve, the tour organizers had booked me on a three-day ferry ride from Vancouver to Prince Rupert, from which I would begin the last half of my tour. They were more than disappointed by my unwillingness to further strand myself on a boat, choosing instead to run around beautiful Vancouver with its active nightlife as a man recently released from incarceration. In fact we had quite a little tug-of-war over the issue. But in this case the artist prevailed, and after three days of R&R in beautiful Vancouver, I flew to Prince Rupert.

On approach for our landing I spotted the ship on which I would have been a passenger disembarking below. While wondering what I might have encountered, I was surprised to notice many ambulances and other emergency vehicles at dockside, and with a closer look, the activity of stretchers and people dressed in white. When we landed I learned that the cruise had encountered a violent three-day storm, resulting in hundreds of sick and dehydrated passengers. Feeling a bit smug about my earlier and lucky stubbornness I was directed to a private portion of the airport where I met my traveling companion for the last three weeks of the tour—a crusty, bearded bush pilot who, as I would soon learn, was primarily aided in the tricky winter wilderness navigation by the whiskey flask in his jacket pocket. Off we went, over the colossal mountains toward three tiny outposts of civilization in northern British Columbia: Terrace, Kitimat, and Smithers.

Descending toward our first destination, we found ourselves with zero visibility in a blinding snowstorm. At this point I discovered my pilot's use of his basic navigational tool, and after a deep swallow he yanked violently back on the stick just as we faced imminent obliteration on the side of an approaching mountain. Over and over we circled and climbed, valiantly looking for any hole in the clouds and the opportunity to touch down. I have no idea how he ever found that runway or the others that followed, for beside his acute personal knowledge of the terrain, there simply was no navigational equipment on the airplane to speak of. Nevertheless, I would learn to trust his instincts, even finding myself enjoying subsequent roller coaster rides in search of holes in the clouds.

Having turned green but at last on *terra firma*, I eased myself from the airplane, holding back a full hour's air sickness with a hand over my mouth, and was greeted by a woman and her two children, all completely covered with snow. After introductions she told me that she had to make an immediate call as we hurried inside to the pay phone. After dialing the number, her only words were, "OK, you can move in the piano. He made it."

Playing With Love

Mannheimer, Genhart, and First Steps to Europe

Mr. Mannheimer was a gentleman in the old tradition. Only in the privacy of his home or in a suite of rooms he kept in London, just off Wigmore Street, did I ever see him dressed less properly than in a jacket and tie. He chose his words with near surgical care and ladled them out slowly, with a deliberateness and measured pace that created a sense of importance in each and every syllable.

I suppose one would have to say that Mr. Mannheimer was not really a famous teacher—not like, for instance, Rosinna Lhevinne at Juilliard—but despite his own disdain for that kind of enterprise or for students that involved themselves in such parasitic adulation, he was regarded with reverence by nearly all who knew and studied with him. One's access to Mr. Mannheimer happened generally before any knowledge of the great man, usually the result of a private recommendation to both teacher and student from someone currently studying with him or one of a number of fine pianists and teachers with whom he had worked over the years. His loyal following had grown person by person over many years, fanning out slowly, like a religious movement gracing an ever-widening family of devotees.

Raised in the Midwest, the first major tragedy of his adolescent life was a flood that ravaged the Mannheimer home, destroying his beautiful Steinway piano. With no assets for its replacement or guidance in what steps to take next in the pursuit of a yet unclear musical goal, this tragedy provided the basis upon which Mr. Mannheimer formed a sturdy personal faith, which would serve him throughout his entire life. This faith was something that was conveyed by the unity of actions and words such as those in one of his favorite maxims: "Preparation is the key to opportunity." For Mr. Mannheimer preparation not only enabled one to both see and to seize opportunities that would otherwise be overlooked, but could actually create opportunity as well. This was what he called "faith in action."

At the border between adolescence and young manhood, a stubborn technical problem demanded an exhaustive pedagogical search concluding in London with the legendary class of the mysterious Tobias Matthay. In stark contrast to the barren expanses of the American Midwest, Mannheimer found himself rubbing shoulders with the likes of the young Clifford Curzon and the immortal Myra Hess, who would become his close personal friend and confidante. At World War II's end, Mannheimer's glowing concert career was cut short due to the slip of a surgeon's knife and the tragic severing of a vital nerve to one arm during a mid-life cancer surgery. In that instant, post-war American audiences lost a great and noble artist whose playing resonated with the rich passion and supreme intelligence that is the legacy of Matthay.

Mannheimer would remain in the United States where his concerts had sent critics stammering for poetic superlatives. But now it would not be the playing itself, but the man, and the warm, vibrant enthusiasm of every mellifluous syllable of his exhaustive and painstaking mission as master teacher. For the lucky few who would move from a seat in the audience to the piano bench of a teaching studio, a listener's awe, once threatened by Mannheimer's private tragedy, now capitulated in a mass following of ardent and able exponents.

Many of America's finest teachers have obediently conveyed the approach in which they themselves were trained. The Russian school was at the center of many renowned studios in New York City's Juilliard School and the Curtis Institute in Philadelphia. But at some major centers and universities, exponents of the German school or the French school lured young talents and created devoted followings.

This dedication to a pedagogical tradition was understandable, but zeal and loyalty to those roots too often created deafness and even disdain toward other approaches. Almost by definition, America's greatest promise is the opportunity for exposure to all the major European pianistic traditions as the basis for what Mrs. Genhart wisely called the International School. With the vigor of newly wrought disciplines, America has a unique opportunity to breathe sublime freshness into the creation of a wholly new pianistic tradition. It's a worthy goal and one within our abilities; yet, the right balance of stylistic uniqueness in combination with thorough and relentless attention to musical fundamentals remains rare in the extreme.

Mr. Mannheimer's ability to see beyond the tradition of his own teaching and achievement in helping every student to sound utterly unique places him, in my mind, as supremely successful. Away from the piano and music, Mannheimer was endowed with an uncommon and penetrating wisdom. He was interested in, and keenly listened to, the personal matters of his students and followers. He provided somewhat of a father-figure to some, but for others determined to face the enormous challenges in pursuing a professional career, he could provide a true rarity: the role of mentor. Such was his bond from the outset with Alfred Brendel, who communicated and visited constantly until Mannheimer's death.

For his devotees, study in his diminutive summer class held in Duluth, Minnesota, offered an annual get together of returning faithful. Here his unusual practice of working generously with all levels of achievement was in greatest evidence. The issue was one of impact on potential. Despite a wide and obvious range of abilities, all were on equal status. Mr. Mannheimer's approach depended on how he felt we were developing on our own terms. A less accomplished person might earn unusual praise if he felt there was outstanding quality relative to individual experience. Likewise, one considering himself a major player could get well iced or damned by faint praise over a performance demonstrating poor attitude or perhaps the continuing presence of some aspect of playing addressed repeatedly without improvement. His demands were absolutely tremendous. Yet somehow in this good and learned man's hands, one's playing could grow by leaps and in rare ways. Every moment in life was seen as a positive opportunity. Failure, understood and faced properly, could set one free to soar. Mr. Mannheimer's comments following the performances that happened once or twice a week were held in great anticipation. During lessons his tact and patience were all but boundless.

But Mr. Mannheimer was not a saint. His greatness was his humanity and the way he dealt with his own life, as a man. During a private lesson, if he finally got fed up, the genteel flow of exchange could be sharply severed by a sudden, "Damn it, Mark!" The effect was so devastating that it would usually be the last time I'd ever do whatever I had done for the rest of my entire life.

In summer gatherings like these, there always seems to be some sort of class clown. Mannheimer's summer class was no exception: ours was a delightful gal I will call Zoey. She had all the extrovert traits one would hope for in an aspiring musician, but somehow, when she got up to play for a group, these same traits would bedevil her into the most unique performance disasters imaginable. We all took special delight in anticipating, "What's going to happen when Zoey plays tonight?" Year after year, we held our collective breath as she made hash in ways that transcended description and defied our imaginations. She wasn't incapable of playing well—often sounding fine through her practice room door. But in front of an audience, Zoey lapsed into creative entanglements that left any empathetic pianist in the audience breathless and terrified to the point of prayer, should it be contagious.

However, after several summers of diligently delivered disasters, Zoey performed one evening without a hitch of any kind. She would have received a standing, even a screaming, ovation from the seventy-five or so students and onlookers in regular attendance except that such a demonstration, although heartfelt, would have been thoroughly and unintentionally insulting as it would ultimately have been perceived as overkill in light of her previous record. When we were all done ushering the flabbergasted Zoey back to her seat following her triumph and the applause had died down, there was a collective lurch in the room as we all silently realized that it would be inconceivable for Mr. Mannheimer, prior to announcing the next player and work, not to christen Zoey's achievement with some inimitable comment.

People lived and died in those classes over the expectation of what the guru-like Mannheimer might say following a performance. Though

Mannheimer, Genhart, and First Steps to Europe 41

we all laughed nervously about it, most of us felt that for one reason or another if you could play for this group in little Duluth, Minnesota, you could play anywhere in the world. For some reason that little class was simply the most nerve-racking place in all Christendom in which to perform.

The previous year, Zoey's offering during a class project of examining and performing the Chopin Etudes was a performance of the delicate and delightful study nicknamed the Butterfly Etude. Anticipating her own record affinity for disaster in performance, she must have practiced this Etude only in tempos so slow and with such morbid diligence and deliberateness that these exaggerated efforts to avoid inevitable derailment resulted in a performance of such ponderous thundering, that the two-page lilting piece we all remembered was all but buried.

Determined to avert a breakdown, Zoey had inadvertently but thoroughly destroyed the very piece she set out to play. And following this monumental performance, as a confused group timidly applauded, Mr. Mannheimer finally pulled himself up, heaved a deep sigh, and uttered, "Well, Zoey, I think we're going to have to rename that *The Giant Moth Etude*." Even he could not restrain from shaking in laughter with the rest of us. To her credit, and with the undying affection of the class, Zoey went right along and was more than a good sport.

But now, what would he say about a performance during which no disaster nor breakdown had occurred and which had all the best intentions of the piece in evidence as well? We all waited in rapt suspense as Mr. Mannheimer slowly rose before the class. We collectively knew that something defining the moment would be coming…but what? Finally, with profound introspection in evidence, Mr. Mannheimer looked slightly heavenward as if sensing some great truth: "Zoey, tonight you have shown us that you are on the very *brink* of musicianship."

With that, those who thought she'd been given a compliment began applauding frantically. Zoey smiled triumphantly, nearly in tears of relief to have earned such a hard-fought accolade. But a whole bunch of us were not so sure it was a compliment. As this love-fest for Zoey went on around us, we re-quoted Mr. Mannheimer's remark, mouthing it silently in dismay to each other over and over until, exhausted with our own exercise in confusion, we finally relegated the truth of the matter to Mr. Mannheimer himself and happily joined in on the rambunctious applause. Knowing that people can only learn that which they are ready to know, Mr. Mannheimer had diplomatically ducked the matter.

In my opinion, little in human nature is stranger than the dynamics of a group of people who spend time with each other on a regular basis. Like most classes at university schools of music or in the private sector, this class in Duluth was no exception: there always seem to be at least one or two complete jerks who fail to understand that there are only two levels of existence in such a situation. Whether during a lesson, at a meeting of the whole class, or over lunch with just a few, there is only the level of the teacher and the level of everyone else. Nevertheless, there always seem to be people indulging in mind-boggling maneuverings attempting to deny that reality.

Mr. Mannheimer thoroughly hated, loathed, and despised any kind of grasping for attention or status, or any other attempt to maneuver one's image in a way to impress others. It is ironic that in literally a matter of days after his death, the long distance phone lines rampaged with a virtual stampede of claims and counterclaims by several of the more ambitious of his students, each claiming to be the heir apparent to the summer class if not the outright successor in general.

Among the greatest, Frank Mannheimer was utterly unique as well—defying not only replacement but even a successor. Although he taught in great detail, Mannheimer had a flawless sense of the balance required between detail and large scale musical ideas that must be maintained to achieve great playing. He said, "The long line (the piece as a whole) is achieved by the absolute understanding and projection of the details." This is not to suggest the importance of one over the other, but rather a perfect balance of the two considerations. I believe it infers that we arrive at the ability to perform the piece as a unit, projecting it as an entity by a thorough study which begins at the cellular level and grows organically in ever larger units toward an inevitable, single structured musical organism. In creating authenticity along with the development of a personal style, one must thoroughly understand this idea and pursue it vigorously.

Genuine musical interpretation is not simply laid over a work like a coat of varnish or point of view. An interpretation, though utterly individual—as each of us perceives and projects even the tiniest morsel of reality with uniqueness—grows with musical and aesthetic purity from the very genes and chromosomes of the piece. The power and the authenticity of a performance is therefore the natural result of study, mastery, understanding, and love in its broadest form. It is not a matter of packaging or otherwise manipulating the end result to impress or otherwise draw attention to one's uniqueness or abilities.

This approach to tackling and performing a piece of music, while requiring an almost selfless sense of simplicity and directness in one's own playing, requires as well a tremendous amount of personal courage, even faith, if you will—faith that somehow, by a sincere effort to simply demonstrate the music itself, one's connection to the listener will be riveting and one's artistic uniqueness will be rightly perceived as authentic, resulting from purity of process and intent.

Just like the great composers themselves, the great performing artists are almost instantly recognizable, their powerful personalities revealed in every moment. This level of playing possesses a simple rightness—a sense in some cases of having nearly composed the work—a sense of it actually bordering on recreation.

Because music is rather like one of the particles newly discovered in physics (existing only in the moment), the doing of it is quite difficult. In order to achieve the needed transparency to reveal not only distinct levels of time but the basic stuff of each—as if looking down through the surface of a very deep pool through all the various layers—success depends on a state of mind, married to body, married to moment—a level truly transcendent of one's abilities. It is a problem of intellectual complexity all but defying description. Every instant of music-making demands consideration and response to all that has gone before, as well as anticipation to all that is coming. Achieving this union is difficult in the extreme. Practice is in fact a matter of creating the opportunity and the ability to respond as an agent of the music in the moment, utterly dependent on a heightened state in which mind, body, music, study, and the moment of performance itself, are all united. Mr. Mannheimer described this state as one of "relaxed concentration." In it, a kind of playing, with a selfless enthusiasm resulting from consummate study, is combined with the special and courageous joy of sharing—sharing that which one loves, lovingly, with those who share that love. For the performer, fully prepared, extraordinary things can and do happen.

When one's being can, for a time, become a living part of the music itself, no physical gesture, no breath of air, no motion, no thought is other than part of the flow of the music. At its best, a fine work of classical music exists in our midst only as it is brought to life by a fine performing artist. In that sense, the composer does not exist without the performing pianist. Our job, our mission as pianists, is to be thoroughly up to the task.

Dwarfed by the genius of a fine composer, on our artistic knees, approaching on a work-by-work basis, with the wits of a scientist, the grace of a ballet dancer, and the daring of a tightrope walker, we can rise above our limits, finding both our meaning and our way forward in the faith that something worthy of love is also worthy of sharing. As children face their limits and find their place in the world through their dreams, adults go on to forge their better selves through the labor of their hands guided by heart and mind.

———•———

To follow Oberlin, I was honored to be invited to study with the great Leon Fleisher, who had heard me as a jury member of the Cliburn Competition. Wisely, John Perry suggested I consider waiting a bit in order to seize the chance to catch a year of graduate school study with the legendary Mrs. Genhart at the Eastman School of Music in Rochester prior to her imminent retirement.

I explained this to Fleisher, who approved of the plan and would welcome me anytime in the future. Difficult as the choice was, the astonishing uniqueness and application of Mrs. Genhart's teaching would go to the very foundation of my playing with huge impact on my future development.

~ ~ ~

Results from great early training are often stunning, but some innate abilities surpass even the best training to the point of being almost freaky. Mrs. Genhart was the younger daughter of the renowned Gottfried Staub. Not only one of the most sought after teachers in Europe, Staub was a huge pianist boasting to have played every work of Franz Liszt—an awesome achievement even for Liszt himself. As Mrs. Genhart told it, she was not only neglected but even belittled by her father, who was stubbornly more devoted to the early showing of her older sister.

During a self-imposed hiatus in his concert activities, the great Ferruccio Busoni took up residence upstairs in the Staub house while he and Staub went through the bulk of his concert repertoire. While there, he took an interest in the neglected younger daughter and began to help Cecile along with her piano lessons. Mrs. Genhart, by her own admission, was not a gifted sight-reader or one possessed of great speed in learning, but as she told me, "Slow as a turtle I was, but once I had a piece, I had it."

In those days, early training was about understanding the rudiments of harmony, transposition and the like. Even small pieces were taught more from the composer's point of view than they are today. Under Busoni, in not much time young Cécile was playing most of the Preludes and Fugues of the Bach W.T.C. and the Chopin Etudes, in any and all keys. Mrs. Genhart liked to tell a story about the level to which her abilities along these lines evolved. It seems that a bit of daydreaming during a performance caused her to accidentally begin Beethoven's Sonata Op. 78 in F# Major in the key of A-flat Major by mistake. Not wanting to reveal her error, she then played the remainder of the work in A-flat! For fun, after telling me this story, she played large sections of Op. 78 for me in several other keys. I sometimes felt a bit inadequate in the presence of such awesome ability. Once when expressing a bit of intimidation to Mrs. Genhart, she dismissed her amazing abilities of transposition as a "knack." Relentlessly demanding, she was also equally complimentary, somehow making playing to her possible.

When Cécile was a young woman, she made her debut in Berlin

playing the Beethoven 1st and Brahms 2nd with the great pianist Edwin Fischer conducting. She studied and traveled for years with Fischer, improvised with Dalcroz in Paris, and performed a large and diverse repertoire throughout Europe to great acclaim from the press and musical public. With training that reflected the utmost in German discipline and thoroughness, the playing of her heyday was never described as having the kind of restrained, even stoic approach suggested in recordings of Kempff or the granite-like Wilhelm Bachaus. Instead, a feel for her playing can be sensed from the color and surging imagination of the mysterious Edwin Fischer himself. Those who witnessed Genhart's mastery marveled at the huge organ-like tone that seemed to ooze out of the piano. Her ease with a miniature or grasp of an epic-scale work was equaled by a vast technical arsenal that possessed reserves of control ranging from the slowest tempo to breathtaking and luminous flight. This kind of expressive range and freedom can only succeed to such a level of rightness when the underlying structural truth is both completely understood and somehow conveyed, even in the most seemingly impetuous performance.

Mrs. Genhart's lifelong approach, emphasizing the mind and reason of the composer, also pops up in startling changes, adorning and personalizing works of which we know every note. By her own admission, later in life and at a different musical time to be sure, she would not so indulge. But to hear her scintillating departures in a remaining recording of the Beethoven First Concerto makes one gasp in surprise and delight in envy and respect for an artist whose grasp of issues fully justifies heavenly little excursions not permitted to mere mortals. She remains, to my mind, possessor of the finest musical ear I have encountered. By virtue of their age, background and abilities, Mrs. Underwood, Mr. Mannheimer, and Mrs. Genhart were no less than living links to the great tradition of pianists. My connection to them was a special blessing.

Over a meal with the artist manager Jacques Leiser, he asked who my favorite pianists were. Frankly, it's a little bit of a test question. But with no thought whatsoever, I said, "Why, they're all dead." Richter had told him the very same thing. Now I'm not comparing my opinion to Richter's; I'm making a quick point about the tradition of which I speak and its importance.

Mrs. Genhart never indulged in the kind of self-adulation evidenced when older and venerable female master teachers of the piano are called "Madame," as in "Madame Lhevinne," "Madame Vengarova," for example. Nevertheless, for the nearly fifty years that she reigned over the Eastman piano department and created a legacy of fine artists stationed atop university programs all over the country, there was never a doubt about the formidable power she wielded or the respect she commanded and deserved.

For ten years running, Mrs. Genhart was the chairman of the Fullbright selection committee, a coveted annual award which sponsored study in Europe for a select group of talented young artists. The annual auditions were held in New York City. It was at the reception following one of them that the ambitious Elena Kobosh, whose students had again failed to be named as among the recipients, approached Mrs. Genhart in a bit of a snit. As they were introduced, Genhart said, "Hello, my name is Mrs. Genhart, how do you do?"

The reply was, "Howwwwww do you dooooooo, I am Madame Kobosh," sending a limp hand adrift in Genhart's general direction.

As Mrs. Genhart told the story, Kobosh was more than a little agitated and launched into a poorly concealed harangue about the fact that after several years she had still failed to have a student selected. On and on she went, peering down at the diminutive Mrs. Genhart as she got more and more angry. Finally, Kobosh decided that she would take the matter to the chairman of the Fullbright committee himself with a protest. With that, she impatiently queried Genhart saying, "Who is the chairman of the committee? I must speak with him. I will wait no longer!"

A bit sheepishly, Mrs. Genhart peered up from behind her glasses and remarked, "Well, Madame Kobosh… I am the chairman of the Fullbright selection committee, and *I* have been for ten years."

Without so much as a millisecond's faltering, Kobosh drew upward into a lofty posture with a forced smile and replied, "Call me Elena."

Near the beginning of my study with Mrs. Genhart at Eastman, I brought in the "Hammerklavier" Sonata of Beethoven. My lessons on that mighty work were a turning point in my musical life. After the slow movement, perhaps the most extensive and profound utterance in all of Beethoven, she said softly to me, "Mein Gott! You have really suffered." Then, going beyond the boundaries of pianist and teacher, she spoke to me about my life with the wisdom of a counselor and doctor. This and other conversations helped me to capture and reveal my true nature and feelings in my playing.

In the next semester, I played my Masters' Recital at Eastman: the Bach E minor Partita, Schubert Dances, and Beethoven's "Hammerklavier" Sonata. A bit stern, I'll admit. Afterward there was a party at my place. I rode to my apartment with Mrs. Genhart. Unfortunately, she was at the wheel—a situation which would have dwarfed any anxiety I may have had about the treacherous fugue to the "Hammerklavier."

The next morning at seven, after a night that had gone on and on, the phone rang. In a stupor, I answered to hear Mrs. Genhart saying that she'd barely slept because of the excitement and went on about the performance and the party. Then she asked me what I would bring to my lesson in two days. Not fully awake, I covered my yawning mouth before answering. Aghast, she exclaimed that I had yawned over the phone at her. Now, I was wide awake and apologizing over and over. Two days later, after playing about eight measures at my lesson, I was stopped and ruthlessly torn to pieces. How dare I bring a piece to her studio in such shabby condition. And I was roundly thrown out.

The next day I received a note to come and see her. I knocked on her door and was greeted in a mixed tone of anger and sorrow. She explained that it was all a result of my yawning over the phone at her. Well, she'd taken me back, and who was I to ignore the cue? After sheepishly entering the studio for my next lesson things were soon back to normal.

On my first recital tour of Europe, I went first to Zurich to see Mrs. Genhart, who had just retired after forty-seven years at Eastman and had returned to the country of her birth. When I brought my program to her, the challenge was mainly that I settle down and just play. I must have sounded more than determined to take Europe by storm. She was her unpredictable self during lessons, vacillating from touching warmth and stupefying insight, to impatient slaps on my back, none of which I ever minded.

After performances in London, Oslo, Amsterdam, and Brussels, I came back to Zurich to play in Town Hall. Mrs. Genhart was very excited. American composer Donald Keats, with wife and three impossible children, were in Fountainebleau with Donald on sabbatical. The day of the recital, there was an awful blizzard through which Keats drove, determined not to miss the Swiss premiere of his big Sonata. We all found each other late that afternoon and wondered if anyone would come through what was literally feet of snow. But the Swiss don't mind a little snow, and the place was jammed. That night, I played my best and was really delighted by the reception. Keats was called up to the platform for several bows for his brilliant Piano Sonata, which had closed the first half of the program.

The evening was magical until, in my dressing room, Mrs. Genhart appeared. She was very happy with me, but nearly drained by the excitement of the night. Then she suggested we go out for dinner. When I reminded Mrs. Genhart that Keats and his wife were also here, the other and very mysterious side of my beloved Mrs. Genhart appeared. She would not have it. This was *her* night; at least ours—just ours. It would be just the two of us. No Keats. No anybody.

A few years down the road, I may have been able to find a diplomatic solution to it all, but then I was a little dumbstruck. Keats came backstage, high as a kite. I explained my problem and begged his forgiveness. He was very kind and seemed to know what was going on. We would meet the next morning.

The dinner Mrs. Genhart arranged was in fact for her students and the most prominent of the local teachers and pianists, Walter Frye, whom she was eager to impress. I felt a little ashamed, thinking of Donald in the hotel after his heroic drive and our big success together.

Mrs. Genhart was one of the very best, with a level of understanding beyond most of us. Like all great teachers, she gave all she had. As always with true greatness, the lessons of her wisdom came from her heart. No great lesson can simply be bought and paid for. It is a gift, a kind of secret imparted with a special understanding. It must be one of love—the shared love of the music and the art of playing—as well as a special kind of love resulting over time between teacher and student. Often Mrs.

Genhart said, "Giving is living!" (pronounced "Geeving ees leeving").

When I arrived at the farthest outpost of Cold War Europe, the landscape seemed as bleak and cold as the weather. Berlin is a city in which one never forgets history. The sobering remains of bomb-shattered buildings linger awkwardly like gravestones. After checking into my hotel, I put on two of everything to deal with the biting cold and headed for the Steinway store. There I knocked on a tiny door under a little curved roof. It swung open, revealing a spherically shaped woman. Her face was round with two apple-like cheeks, and her hair was pulled back into a tight round bun. From the neck down were more spheres, with sturdy short legs and pudgy feet to hold up this stout column of various fruits and melons.

"Ach! Meester Vestcott. I am Frau Schwäggermann." she sung out in mellifluous tones of a typically German mixture of genuine warmth with a pride and professionalism that seemed at once to say, "I'm delighted to meet you—don't mess with me."

As she showed me around the store and warehouse, she offered that if the piano at the Hochshüle für Musik wasn't to my liking, I could have any I liked. I practiced only an hour on passage work, one or two themes, and some bits that hadn't seemed quite right in Zurich. When I finished, Frau Schwäggermann invited me for a typical German businessman's lunch.

I'm not very sensitive about my diet on a concert day, but this meal proved fatal: some awful boiled pigs' shanks with sauerkraut, red cabbage, potato pancakes, and a bottle of beer. I returned to the hotel and slept until late afternoon. After dressing and a brisk walk to the Hall, I warmedup onstage before the audience was admitted. Returning to my dressing room, the usual butterflies of pre-concert nerves were starting to flutter around in my stomach. What followed was a little more than just butterflies. Between multiple trips to the restroom, I anxiously paced around my dressing room, desperately trying to expel what seemed a dirigible-sized baffle of gas. When it became past time to play the crew finally insisted I begin.

With all the control I could muster, I walked on stage. Probably no one at my Berlin debut would have suspected that I was exploding inside with laughter (among other things), over what felt like imminent disaster. As I began the elegant severity of the Partita, as if on cue, my rumblings demanded their moment as well. I played on, knowing that total denial of nature would have catastrophic consequences. For the next thirty minutes, all choreographed to the magnificent outpouring of Bach, I leaned slightly this way and that, playing a little louder here and there. I even took a repeat of the Sarabande, nearly *forte throughout.*

Fortunately, I did finally settle down and the rest of the program was a sheer delight to play. I felt as if that audience hung on every note I played. At the conclusion of the Brahms Sonata the hall went absolutely wild, with a standing ovation such as I had never received, people cheering—some even rushed forward to the edge of the platform, extending their hands to me. It went on and on and was really heaven.

Back in my dressing room, Frau Schwäggermann appeared with the local manager and his staff. They were gushing with excitement, telling me that what had happened was most unusual.

"Well, let's go out to eat," I said looking forward to an after-concert dinner which I could order for myself. But one by one, each faded out with the prospect of another day's work. I was driven back to my hotel and left to celebrate my triumphant night alone. As I flopped face-down on the bed, the sound of my heart pounding, I wondered if I'd ever manage to sleep. I've never been lonelier than on that funny and dazzling night in Berlin.

The next morning, I arrived on schedule at the office of the local manager. "Well," he said, "You've had a triumph in Berlin," and presented me with reviews from two morning papers. The critic in *Die Welt* said that my Bach was "immersed in tender forms and swimming colors" and that "it was a performance which put [me] in a league with Wilhelm Kempff." I briefly mused on whether I had accidentally stumbled onto Kempff's dietary secrets. Luckily, the reviews from other cities on that tour were as good. I began to understand the value of my labors under the living links who were my teachers.

Frank Mannheimer and Cécile Genhart never actually met in person, but over many years they sent students back and forth to each other. Their personalities, backgrounds, and teaching styles were as different as night and day. One could go nuts studying a big, difficult work with one followed by the other. Often, the demands of one were the exact opposite of the other.

Miraculously, they both summed up the basis of study in exactly the same way: that the "long line", that is, the unified or overall success of the entire piece, was achieved by the absolute understanding and projection of the details. It is not hard to imagine, therefore, that much of their teaching was enormously detailed at the most exacting level imaginable. However, in both, there was an uncanny knack of maintaining just how all this detail added up to the sum of the piece as a whole.

With both teachers one understood the organic union which relates every detail of the piece to its part or role in the progression of the piece in its entirety. Interpretation evolved almost organically as one grew in his awareness, layer by layer, from one scale of understanding toward the other. This perfect relationship between the big and the small in a composition is not only the signature of a great composer but is the essence of a quality performance itself. In my opinion, the mastery of this balancing act, and its ultimate projection to an audience, is at the very heart of great playing as well as success with the public.

Despite the attributes of natural excitement or a sense of bravura in the playing, when too many details are swept under the rug and the forward drive or impetuosity is relied upon too much, the playing will lack depth of feeling, or individuality. However, if details become too important, eventually the playing can sound stiff, mannered, and the natural flow or inner excitement essential in carrying listeners along through a large work can falter. I call this the school of bows and ribbons. At first one thinks, "Oh my, what a sensitive and musical player." But by intermission, the playing can start to sound to the listener as if the artist is actually inspecting his own playing rather than succumbing to the demands of the work as a whole. Lacking in abandon, this kind of playing fails with the public for just the opposite reason as that of the other.

Good playing comes from daily practice which is both attentive to drive and big ideas on one hand, with finesse and the mastery and projection of small moments on the other. Too much of one and you lose excitement, and your audience, right along with it. Too much of the other and you lose the purpose which rests at the heart of any fine work of music—its humanity and the lingering moment of that potent musical hunch which led to its creation.

Playing With Love

That's 'Hol-l-l-ywood,' with Three or Four L's!
—Bullwinkle J. Moose

"In life, as in business, when you make a mistake, buy your ass out of it as fast as possible. Don't try to turn it into something that wasn't a mistake." Characteristically blunt and earthy, J. M. Johnson recited to me one of his cardinal rules.

I wish I'd followed it.

With my Master's Degree from Eastman in hand I was now receiving sporadic invitations to play here and there at generally low fees. This was perhaps the most difficult time of my professional life. In an instant I seemed to have gone from the very top of the heap as student and promising young artist, to nearly the bottom of the heap as burgeoning professional.

Free from academia and the guidance of constant contact with a teacher, I was suddenly determining my own course toward a professional goal at a time when I knew little or nothing about how it could be reached. I could never have imagined the obstacles and disappointments I would face during these years. Only my natural tenacity, my love of what I did, the ongoing encouragement of artists I admired, and my ability for hard work would eventually bring me to my goal.

During this period, having returned to the family home in Portland, I received a call from the director of the Young Musician's Foundation in Los Angeles. In their eyes I'd done pretty well since winning the Debut Award as a teenager. She went on to explain a new YMF strategy: a management program for a few former winners to get them playing in the L.A. area. After all, with over two dozen orchestras, and God knows how many recitals, the YMF was well placed to promote and book promising alumni around L.A., which could serve as a stepping stone to national management in New York City.

It was a great idea. Another pianist and I, along with a violinist and a cellist, were to be the first young artists in the program. I was asked to move to L.A. post haste. Shortly after arriving, I began what became weeks of phone calls trying to connect with the suddenly elusive director. When I did reach her in Palm Springs, I was tersely told that the whole thing was off. No excuses. No explanation. No nothing. And there I was, with even less. My mistake was made. I should have left right then for New York City, but naive and in shock, I stubbornly and stupidly festered in L.A. purgatory.

Meanwhile, a bitter divorce settlement, which now embroiled my European manager in Amsterdam, unexpectedly threatened to dismantle all the plans for my return to Europe. There seemed no reason not to enter the Tchaikovsky Competition in Moscow. With a bit less than a year, I pulled out my score to the Tchaikovsky Concerto first thing.

With my application, I needed a letter of recommendation. While at Eastman I had played for the great Russian pianist Vladimir Ashkenazy in a master class. I was thrilled that he had liked my playing very much and that a lively correspondence between us had continued ever since. I decided to ask Mr. Ashkenazy for my recommendation, and some weeks later I received word from Moscow that all necessary forms and letters had arrived and that I was accepted.

During this time in L.A., I had a wonderful loft over an auto mechanic shop in Pasadena with the most beautiful acoustics imaginable. There was a huge expanse of beams and skylights, all divided by panels of sweeping scrim. Nearly every day, the beautiful L.A. sunsets would pour through a dozen windows creating a prism of color throughout. However, artsy lifestyle aside, my life in Los Angeles was stuck in a rut. Vacillating between anger and optimism, bitterness and false pride, I began to feel trapped.

Through a friend, and after tremendous buildup, I met the actress Ellen Burstyn. There was no denying that the prospect of knowing a few movie people gripped me with some interest. However, I also began to feel a little foolish, receiving lots of false praise from people who knew zip about my work and cared less.

During this time I met Rashad. From England, he was a Sufi master and on the scene in L.A. for the first time. Ellen, known as Hadia by her Sufi friends, was one of a small group of Sufi movie-folk that had invested considerable time, effort, and money in bringing Rashad to America. If Satan was trying to collect souls in this nutty environment, in contrast, Rashad was there to save them, setting some free from a collective professional madness to become the directors of the ongoing movies of their own lives.

He was indeed a holy man, with an unassuming manner but an unwavering sense of mission as well. His sharp English wit and general personal gusto contrasted dramatically with the special reverence in which he was held by those knowing the unique personal power he possessed. Accounts circulated of spectacular metaphysical or, if you prefer, paranormal events in which he played a role. However, such accounts were only whispered, never portrayed as matters demanding full acceptance. And that was as it should have been. Rashad, like his message, was about the present and the future that would grow intrinsically from it.

Part of his appeal was his modesty, his humility, even his normalcy. Likewise, no conspicuous payments or personal sacrifices were required of his supporters. Rich in the love and gratitude of many, Rashad lived a simple, even spartan life which glowed with an acute connection to the moment, remaining free of material encumbrances. Whatever or whoever Rashad was, he was not only a truly good man but one of enough genuine power to ignite the paranoiac concerns of the U.S. Federal Immigration people who had put every conceivable roadblock in his journey toward L.A. There is no doubt that any suspicions were not only pure garbage, but could even serve as strong evidence of the man's genuine merits. All too often in the 70s, the litmus test of one's virtues was directly proportionate and opposite to the negative assessment and subsequent difficulties at the hands of totally unenlightened, naive, and thoroughly overzealous bureaucrats loitering throughout government agencies.

Every Wednesday evening there was a meeting in Ellen's large living room attended by about three-dozen of the faithful and newly curious, with a prominent majority of movie professionals. With so many in the movie industry often possessing larger-than-life personalities at the meetings, there often existed the scent of utter determination to achieve and project spiritual enlightenment that completely obscured any genuine peace of mind or introspection, elusive enough in any group situation.

As I was confronted by any number of expectations to participate as an active member in what was, to be sure, a genuinely worthy opportunity, I just could not equate my already private tendencies in matters of faith or spirit with an environment of such strong and strange group psychodynamics gripping the Sufi hopefuls that were the norm, not only at meetings but at other social gatherings as well. I've never been a joiner, partly out of shyness and partly because group behavior often just plain embarrasses or confuses me. Despite prodding, I just couldn't attend the meetings.

Perhaps my absence from the flock was one of the reasons a warm friendship between Rashad and me developed over several weeks. Our laughter and frequent outings together did not go unnoticed by those seeing everything near Rashad as a kind of pecking order. Inevitably as my place in the barnyard appeared and enviably elevated, so also was the level of personal contempt in which I was held by many of the faithful.

One night after an out-of-work actress friend of Ellen's had angrily noticed my absence at the meeting, I was prompted to offer a tepid explanation to Rashad for my continuing absence. To my relief, he cut me off saying, "Look Mark, don't be ridiculous. There are no methods and no teachers. There's only life. And when these poor [souls] give up on this, and maybe on me as well, they might have a chance to find what's right under their nose."

Back in Pasadena, I was awakened one night by the most bizarre sounds. My bed was near the front windows, and to the right was a large padlocked trapdoor in the floor covering the descending stairs to the dark mechanic shop below. When I heard the sounds again (and louder) I thought I might not be dreaming. Running the funny little mental checks one does in moments like these to make sure one is in fact not dreaming, the sounds became clearer. This was no dream. A chaotic chorus of voices began to call from beneath the trap door in voices high and low, loud and soft, "Mark, Mark, come with us. Come now." Imploring, then demanding in a hundred ways and a hundred tones, they insisted. I became breathlessly afraid and listened acutely, wishing, waiting for this cacophony to cease.

The instant I realized I could not even move a muscle was a moment of terror beyond description. Either petrified with fear or terrified by my immobility, even my breathing stopped as my body was sliding slowly sideways towards the edge of my bed in the dreaded direction of the trapdoor, which had somehow fully opened. I tried repeatedly to move but remained stone frozen, helplessly unable to lift a finger, still slipping sideways as the sheets gathered up against me. I began to pray, unable even to speak.

Then, suddenly, like the theater marquee, the word will began to flash on and off in red neon in my mind. As it pulsed like an alarm, it struck me that this was truly a battle of will. My life had become such a leaf in the wind—my self-respect you could have flown like a kite—and now I was falling easy prey to some God-knows-what marauding collector of spirits.

Still trying desperately to move, I screamed silently over and over in my mind, "Will! Will!" I fought and wrestled. "I *will* move. I *will*." It may have been a second or a minute, but the agony made it seem nearly forever. Finally, I moved.

Leaping out of bed and away from the gaping trap door, I yelled at the top of my lungs. Racing for a light, I whirled around to see all my bedding bunched up like an accordion. At that moment, the huge trap door slammed shut. I called a friend, who, from the tone of my voice and with no explanation, set a land speed record from West L.A. to Pasadena. For the next few hours we sat in silence until the sun came up.

First thing in the morning, I discussed the ordeal with Rashad. He was deeply concerned, feeling that due to our close friendship, I may have been the target of some kind of predatory presence. I knew in my gut it would be our last meeting, as I was urgently but lovingly instructed on some safeguards should anything like the experience occur in the future.

Moving to L.A. proved to be a mistake when the Young Musician's Foundation's offer was capriciously withdrawn. My mistake was in staying stubbornly on, trying my best with the leftovers of a situation in shambles. The scary experience in my loft was a potent, if surreal reminder of the level of confusion to which my life had descended by not following the simple wisdom of Mr. Johnson's earthy admonition.

It was time to retake control of my own destiny, regardless of how uncertain that may be. The upcoming Tchaikovsky competition in Moscow provided a tangible goal, and New York seemed the obvious place in which to pursue my future. The worst I could do was fail, but even in failure, I would still have my will.

Moscow Intrigues

In New York I lived in a former maid's quarters in the Des Artistes—a very small apartment in a very good building. It cost $75 a month. I practiced at a Baptist church in midtown.

From the competition, Van Cliburn had taken a big interest in my playing. He'd encouraged me to stay in touch with him, and I did. The next time Van was in town, he heard some of my pieces and gave me a smashing lesson on Tchaikovsky's "Dumka". All the contest repertoire was in good shape and comfortable for me, with the exception of a short but difficult new work composed especially for the competition. I hated it and struggled to get it together.

Just a week before I was supposed to leave for Russia, a man with the Institute of International Education at the United Nations called to say there seemed to be a problem. All the American contestants were to travel in a group to Moscow. However, the official list of contestants had just been received, and my name was suddenly *not* on the list. Months before I had heard directly from the competition in Moscow and now found this strange and worrisome. He called back the next day to say he'd spoken to Moscow and there was no record of me.

I called Van. After two nights on the telephone to Russia, he said, "They claimed over and over not to have you. I said it was impossible and finally forced them to admit you. The funny thing is that when I asked about you bringing your press materials along, they said not to bother, they already had them." Then his tone darkened, "Mark, something is wrong. I think it might be best if you didn't go."

I couldn't believe my ears. Nor could I imagine why I alone should be lost in some bureaucratic shuffle. I simply *had* to go. Reluctantly, Van gave me his blessing.

Once in Russia, along with the other contestants, I was introduced to my interpreter and checked into the colossal Hotel Rossia near St. Basil's Church off Red Square. At every corner of every floor sat a formidable looking woman who kept keys and sold drinks and snacks. The food in Russia was just as awful as everyone had said it would be. The first night another contestant and I took off for a Hungarian restaurant that he insisted was the best in Moscow. (He was a Liszt freak and keen on all things Hungarian.) After nearly staging a revolution for a table, a typically grim woman took our orders for Chicken Paprika, the house specialty. An entire hour passed during which we sat dumbfounded by a small orchestra trying to play American jazz favorites for a group of beefy women stubbornly dancing a strange kind of folk-disco in pairs, grasping each others' forearms like Roman gladiators. Sweating like horses, in drab cotton print dresses, these girls were all checking in at 200+ lbs. Their husbands remained alone at the tables getting semi-comatose on vodka. Who would blame them?

It would have been funny if we hadn't by this time become both drunk and starving. I thought we'd died and gone to restaurant hell, a notion confirmed when our meal came: two soup plates were placed on the table, each with one tiny wing, a few shreds of meat and the occasional pinfeather drifting aimlessly in a puddle of pale broth. We finally broke our pretense of diplomacy and asked if there might be something else we could eat—anything! But, of course, no one cared. No one ever cared. Almost every question was answered by "Nyet!" (no). Only from there did the bargaining sometimes begin. For days at a time, stores, as well as our hotel, ran completely out of milk, bread, and even eggs. Only one thing was absolutely never in short supply—vodka. Never! It reminded me of the soma pills in *1984*. Every day at five p.m., Red Square filled with staggering, listing bodies on their daily commute from a bleak job to an even bleaker evening at home.

We returned to the hotel hungry but happy to see the nightly return of the La Scala Opera Company chatting and smoking in groups on the front steps. After an evening's performance at the Bolshoi, their return to the hotel ignited a small piece of Moscow with their friendly chatter and easy smiles.

On my second day in Moscow, I faced several hours of practice in a stifling hot room at the Moscow Conservatory. Not wanting to ruin good clothes practicing, I tossed on a pair of Levi's and a white cotton shirt and headed off past the corner of St. Basil's, along a long wall of the Kremlin, and through Gum, the large department store. Just beyond was a wonderful ice-cream stand that would become a regular stop. On my way there, I became certain I was being followed. And indeed I was, but by an unlikely group of teenage boys. I made my stand at the ice-cream store, carefully choosing a table. The group stopped about twenty feet away and made what appeared to be an agreement among themselves. Then one fellow emerged and meekly approached my table. He spoke English.

"Ve all excoose ourselfes to you vor sach behavior. Baht you see, there iss deal ve might like to do."

"What do you mean?"

"Vell, you see, your levi–pants, are very sought avter here and ve vould like to buy them from you. Ve vant if you vill sell."

I was delighted to comply but not interested in any profit. And in fact, the deal we made for two pairs of American Levi 501s was invaluable during my stay in Moscow. For the next several nights, one of the boys made it his business to take me to a restaurant where I could actually find some good food.

Now my biggest challenge was no longer eating but my American roommate, also in the competition. I had managed to pick a vegetarian who practiced yoga with a vengeance. In the wee hours of my first morning in Moscow I was awakened by the labors of deep-breathing exercises that went on forever. Grasping the last remnants of sleep as if by my fingernails, I lurched fully awake as my roommate performed the finale to his wake-up ritual by sticking his fingers down his throat. With all the diplomacy for which I am known and loved, I put a stop to it by day two. I couldn't get rid of him nor could I move; but like an animal cornered, I was not beyond making a physical threat. The breathing might have been OK, but waiting in a dark room for someone to blow chips every morning was too much.

On the day I played in the first stage, I was of course practicing at the conservatory. It's not exceptional before performances to have some nerves, sometimes a lot of them. Sometimes that can include a case of diarrhea, and God help me, this plagued me in Moscow. With my performance growing near and nature whispering, "Oh no", I hurriedly left my practice studio for the men's bathroom upstairs.

Now a urinal is a urinal. Give me a fancy white one, a granite slab wall, a tray, a tea cup—I don't care. At the Moscow conservatory, a wall with a little water trickling down would have to do. But for more serious and complex maneuvers, even a modicum of equipment and hopefully a bit of comfort is recommended. Yes, indeed there were stalls. But no, there were no doors. There were no toilets either, just a ditch toward the edge of the cement floor with a water tap over it on the wall. What was one to do with a ditch? I was in my only blue suit, in sweltering hot weather, and cursed by a bowel on the warpath. I'd have sold my soul for a kitchen chair, a bush, a log perhaps, a whoopie cushion—anything on which to perch.

Desperate, I undid my fly and began to mentally prepare for a physical maneuver which promised to make my imminent piano performance child's play. Then, at that special moment when one says, "Thank God, I made it." the most awful fact came home: No paper. Nothing. Anywhere. The consequences were unthinkable. I pulled myself together and made a seemingly endless trek back down to my practice studio. Desperate, I dug through my music for something I could sacrifice. Of course. That horrible new piece composed especially for the competition. Nearly paralyzed with cramps and laughter, I labored back upstairs to the men's bathroom to face the ditch from hell.

When I finally played, though it was pretty good, it was not my best. However, the ovation I received was encouraging, and when I walked off stage two men from the Soviet news agency TASS asked me about doing some interviews. Over the next few days, my time with these gentlemen made the best times of my trip to Moscow. They showed me many wonderful things, the best of which was the famed Moscow Circus. Every act was choreographed with the artistry of ballet. Only recently has Cirque du Soleil in Las Vegas begun to compare.

On the day the results of the preliminaries were announced, all the contestants were massed around a man who called out the names of everyone admitted to the second stage. There were a couple dozen judges. A score of 24 was perfect, and an average of 17 was needed to pass on. When my name was not called, lots of other Americans came by to express their shock. Listening to these regrets embarrassed me, so I walked to the hotel after a quick exit.

On arriving I found that all my belongings had been rummaged through. I changed clothes and went downstairs to the bar. There sat one of the men from TASS. He offered to buy me a drink and had a certain expression that urged me to overlook my desire to be alone and accept. Drink after drink followed, except I was washing down food and he was not. With a clear plot to get me smashed, I had suspected earlier that this gentleman's kindness exceeded norms and had been wary that his personal fondness might as well. Before long, hanky-panky was undoubtedly afoot in the Hotel Rossia bar.

I lingered, not due to politeness, but because of just too many mentions of a mysterious black book carried by all the men of TASS. Drink by drink I found out it contained all the scores of the contestants. When my conversational friend dropped that there was an utterly unpianistic explanation for my early elimination from the contest, I thought back to my talk with Van and my sudden exclusion from the list of contestants. He pulled the book from his breast pocket and raised his eyebrows knowingly. My drunken host had fallen nearly helpless into the trap he'd coyly set for me. The time to act had come.

I offered obligingly to help him to his room. Inside the door, I helped him through an outer room to a second and dumped him in a heap on the bed. Helping him off with his jacket, I plucked the key and the black book from his pocket and bolted out of the inner room, locking him in. In those days, Russian hotel-room locks were simply a deadbolt—equally effective at locking one in and keeping intruders out.

Back in my room I pored over the book. I found my name and, much to my surprise, there was not just my average score, but the individual marks of each judge. As I began going down the list, country by country, I was shocked to see that all the scores were 21 or above, with two perfect 24s. But when I reached the half-dozen USSR judges: "3.3.3.3.3.3." These kinds of marks would certainly wreak havoc on an average, and indeed my average was just below the needed 17. I had been blackballed.

My phone rang. My drinking buddy was not a little upset and still quite drunk. I told him to sit tight and shut up. When I returned the book the next morning, he was not amused.

Winding through this already complex adventure was another little problem with the interpreter who had been assigned to me. She was a very nice Jewish girl in her thirties with freckles and an oval-shaped face. From day one, she decided I should be the winner. But I soon learned that she was not so interested in my pianistic potential when she began to talk about her little boy, her ex-husband and that she had well-to-do relatives near Philadelphia, where she also owned a little land. She talked a lot about life in Russia. Although she did not feel the Jews in Russia to be singled out for persecution, this attitude did not prevent her from planning an exit from the USSR with her son.

Over the days she talked more and more poignantly about her hopes for her son's future, about her sister's marriage to a Frenchman and her resulting exit from Russia, and didn't I find her even the least bit attractive? Then she asked me point blank to marry her. Over and over she persisted in asking, "Mark, can't you please find it in your heart to find a way? Please help me and my son. Please."

In fact, the big question had been sprung on me as I was walking back to my hotel from the Conservatory having just been thrown out of the competition. She was relentless, repeatedly promising that the marriage would be annulled as soon as possible.

I felt trapped. I was angry, but not without sympathy for her. During that endless walk back to the Hotel Rossia all I could do was apologize and say "no" repeatedly and firmly as the tears flowed from her drooping face.

In the middle of the night, after I had finished the black book and lay restlessly awake, she called. We talked a long time, and after hanging up, I didn't blame her one bit for giving it her all. What a strange place this was—so much just a means to an end: a competition rigged to get rid of a political undesirable, and a marriage proposal for a visa.

The next day, I boarded the bus for the airport. Right on cue, there was my interpreter, this time with her son, saving a seat for me. My heart sank. In one last desperate try, she began again with the "Why nots?" and "Couldn't you just…," crying all the way to the airport.

As we waved goodbye, I wondered if I was feeling the kind of suspicion and fear that the people in Russia lived with. Grateful just to leave, ironically, I'm sure there were a few people, including that man from TASS, who were glad to see me go.

The moment I arrived in New York, I called up Van. "Come right over," he said, and followed typically with, "We'll have a steak."

When we met he was all consolation and understanding but unusually awkward. I wondered if he was disappointed in me, but I had decided to tell no one about the black book incident and the scores from the Russian judges. In a way, I had been warned and felt uneasy about saying anything that sounded like belly-aching.

Van rose from his chair and walked a few times around the room. "This is more than a hunch, but did Ashkenazy write your recommendation to the contest?"

"Yes."

"My God," he muttered. "For a while I couldn't believe it, but now it all makes too much sense."

"What does?"

"Mark, just a month or two before the contest, Ashkenazy was taken off the official list of previous winners. Ashkenazy did a sort of tell-all interview in the *London Times* in which he was more than critical of much of his training in Russia. I think too, there was a big bru-ha-ha over his family with the Russian government at the same time."

Van then revealed that when Ashkenazy was 'erased' in typical USSR style from the list of previous winners, so was I mysteriously 'lost' from the contest files. It made perfect sense and more than explained six scores of 3 points each from the Russian judges.

During that time Van's kindness to me provided solace, comfort and wisdom. Van possessed an engaging personality, with warmth, a self-effacing wit, and an intelligence not to be underestimated. For these and other reasons, he was loved, and rightly so, all over the world. My visits to Van were always at his suite of rooms in the Salisbury Hotel, but at the time his real home was in Shreveport.

He must have played more than once in the Philippines, for he seemed to have struck up a friendship with Ferdinand and Imelda Marcos. During one of my visits to Shreveport, the recent talk around town was about a party given by a wealthy resident who had managed an appearance by Imelda Marcos. Months after the affair, people who hadn't managed an invitation were still grumbling. But for those more fortunate, another adventure awaited.

The next season during my visit to Shreveport, I learned that Mrs. Marcos, in gratitude for the party, chartered two full-sized jets and flew several hundred people from the previous year's affair to New York City for several days, putting them all up at the Plaza, the St. Regis and the like. By this time, the people who had been grumbling about being left out before were fuming with indignation over the social, financial, and even moral excesses of what must have been no less than a routine social expense for the woman whose appetite for good footwear seemed only the tip of the iceberg.

Being in Van's presence was to be immediately warmed by his huge success. During a visit I often felt a bit astonished by the whole whirlwind of his life: his next concert, the hours of frantic practice sandwiched in between, and a constantly ringing phone. Suddenly, for one reason or another, I was grabbed by the arm and we'd dash out full-throttle across a six-lane rampage of non-stop traffic. Since his code of politeness did not allow for keeping others waiting, ignoring a detail such as trekking to a corner crosswalk, Van's system was simply to hold his head up recognizably high, grab his companion firmly by the hand and charge forward through the squealing brakes, honking horns, and even louder profanity.

Following one such successful crossing which ended next to the open door of a large, black limousine in which his mother was waiting because, as Van said, "She'll want to say 'hi' to you," I was unceremoniously pushed in head first. Unable to daintily maneuver, I fell in a heap onto the lap and into the arms of a lady who was not Van's mother. My senses first alerted me to her very expensive perfume. That was my introduction to Imelda Marcos. When Van got in, with no other place to roost, I put on my most nonchalant air and tried to do whatever one is supposed to do in polite conversation while sitting on the lap of the wife of a head-of-state.

My exit from this ordeal was choreographed by the driver to happen curbside, directly in front of the door of the very busy Patelson's Music Shop. I've never regretted a bit of notoriety more than at the moment the door flung open and I exited amid hugs and kisses from Mrs. Cliburn and Mrs. Marcos, in front of what seemed to be at least one thousand dazed pianists, many of whom were friends or acquaintances of mine.

Behind any fine artist, one finds at least one person indispensable to their success. Van's mother was very much involved in all of his activities, dealing with management and arranging his concert schedule, while providing help at home with all the little things of day-to-day life. She was an unforgettable character. Loving, effusive, almost giddy with enthusiasm, she could easily be underestimated. She was one of the finest teachers anywhere and the mother and mentor of a great artist. A friend of mine witnessed first-hand a remark typical of the surprising candor of her folksy but unimpeachable wisdom. At a reception following an all-Liszt recital in sleepy little Tyler, Texas played by Van on a sweltering, humid afternoon, there was a bit of grumbling about "all that Liszzzt!" from some less sturdy patrons. Her temperature rising with the comments, Mrs. Cliburn exclaimed, "Fiddle-dee-dee, what's all this complain'n 'bout Liszzzt? Why the reason most pianists don't like Liszzzt is 'cause they just cayn't *play* 'im."

Playing With Love

Good Isn't Bad
—Just Not Enough

Not long after returning from Moscow, I was invited for a midday benefit cocktail party just north of town on the grounds of a lovely estate. On that lucky day I met the great American composer, Samuel Barber. On that day also, Mr. Barber introduced me to Bob Brown, a pianist of some ability and a socialite par excellence in and around New York City.

Looking like Albert Finney in *Tom Jones*, this pianistic and social tornado had stormed up and down the East Coast playing the piano and breaking as well the hearts of many women. From Barber to Brown, and then from Brown, I was soon introduced to the manager of Town Hall, with the emphatic directive of my consideration to be presented in a New York debut recital.

Bob didn't waste a minute; nor did he bother to hear me play prior to the introduction. However, the next day I did play for the manager of Town Hall, who decided on the spot that I would be the first young artist in thirteen years to be presented by Town Hall itself. Concerned about an audience, I agreed to use the services of a public relations firm and pay for printed material and a Times ad in addition to the Hall's efforts. For this I applied for and received a very unusual grant from the Martha Baird Rockefeller Fund for Music. The next summer I pulled together a program suitable for the tests of a New York debut:

1) **BACH** — Chromatic Fantasy and Fugue.
2) **BRAHMS** — Variations on an Original Theme, Op. 33A, a mid-sized work of color and tenderness, musically challenging and a strong contrast to the Bach.

3) **DONALD KEATS** — Piano Sonata, that I had played in Europe—a relatively unknown work that would draw critics, with great range and large scale.

INTERMISSION

4) **SCHUBERT** — Sixteen Dances, a group of short waltzes, contrasting miniatures on a power-house program, stylistically demanding.

5) **RAVEL** — "Gaspard de la Nuit", three pieces, a consummate test of technical, coloristic and stylistic issues of French music—a work of renowned and transcendent difficulty.

My friends here and there, members of faculties or the local music teachers' association, got the plea that I needed to try the program wherever possible. After Christmas, playing it several times on the West Coast, I began to work my way across the country.

This period in New York City was spent in tandem with a lovely gal named Liz. She was a good pianist and a great pal. We shared an apartment on West 90th Street a half block from the park just behind the El Dorado. On the weekends the lovely tree-laden street even smelled of horse manure, with Manhattan's only existing stables a couple of blocks west. Believe me, it sounds odd, but somehow the smell of horse manure can be almost pleasant in the New York environment.

I loved living in New York, and I still believe that it should be required of every young person to spend at least one season there as a part of their general education. Liz and I got a lot of education. We fielded problems for each other, were often on each other's arm, and occasionally in them, and flourished in a daily routine punctuated by a quiet "be careful" followed by a quick kiss. We helped each other grow up a lot, were fiercely loyal, and could not be subverted.

People often see in others that which they want to see. Along that line Liz and I were lucky. Both blond, Liz did not tower over my then male average height of 5'8", unlike an increasing number of young women in recent years. In truth this has never been of any importance to me then or now, other than sparing me the occasional crick in my neck following a long evening.

On our adventures Liz and I quickly learned what I have held firmly to be true ever since: that New York City has the most helpful, generous, and truly kindhearted people anywhere. More than once, on an excursion to a better than average restaurant, Liz and I would discover that a nearby couple had quietly paid for our dinner, slipping out even before we might have been introduced or said, "Thank you".

Liz and I were veterans of standing room for the ballet and opera, the elimination of which by many houses around the country in recent years I consider to be a crime against humanity. Just a little attention to our attire and a few minutes chatting outside the door and holding a small sign, reading, "tickets?" often resulted not only in the chance to buy a leftover seat inexpensively but more often, a pair of really expensive seats given freely with a warm smile. We saw everything.

Occasionally, following a rough day or a big disappointment for one of us we'd wear a different kind of hat and go to one of the big discos, like Studio 54, which were beginning to pop up around town. While high-style 'wanna-be's' froze anxiously in a line down the block, we made sure that our cab delivered us right in front of the door where we were usually warmly welcomed by the staff, instantly whisked inside like royalty. Once, as the velvet rope was being pulled aside, a nearby line-dweller whispered, "They must be somebody…."

Liz and I provided for each other a sense of home with the trust, protection, and frank discourse of fiercely loyal friends. From this safety we pressed forward our separate professional and social forays, sharing the details with each other during nightly aural diaries.

With the total surprise which was the norm of my life at that time, my lifestyle took a giant leap forward when a friend of mine, who was about to move to California for a fine new job he had landed, asked me if I would like to take over his role as escort to a well-known model. At that time her great beauty, personal charm, and professional savvy had catapulted her to a position of great professional and social demand. To these assets was added an uncommon intelligence and a gregarious personality.

Suddenly, once or twice a week I found myself in a chauffeur-driven car in tandem with a world-class beauty whose circle of friends and social favorites included famous artists, living legends of New York show business, and celebrities of all kinds. My responsibilities ranged simply from being good company with diligent attention to her needs, safety and comfort, to adroit handling of any potentially awkward situation. The arrangement provided for her safety as well as the peace-of-mind of her husband, whose busy business schedule demanded constant travel away from New York City.

Our very first evening together began by meeting up with our dinner entourage over cocktails in the Oak Room of the Plaza Hotel. On my toes, trying to stay as cordial and relaxed as possible in the company of my new responsibility, we were joined by Leonard Bernstein, Adolph Green, creator of many Broadway hits including *Gypsy*, Broadway performer and TV personality Phyllis Newman, all topped off with artist legend, Salvador Dali, complete with his trademark mustache, magnificent walking cane and remarkably sturdy wife at his side.

The only conceivable way to have expanded in any recognizable measure on the luster of the people at hand was to have proceeded from the great to the greatly ridiculous. To that end the evening's group was topped off by one of Dali's favorites: an unlikely, if not downright surreal personality around town as well as Fire Island, the 6-foot-plus black drag queen known as Potassa. In the privacy of our car en route to mid-town's fabulous L'Aurandt restaurant, my new companion and I cemented the happy tone and private candor that would endure between us by referring to Potassa as 'Potato.' For the rest of the evening over a sumptuous dinner and all the trimmings we shared the quiet agony of two otherwise civil people trying desperately not to laugh out loud over our secret.

The evening also provided my first appearance in the society section of the New York Times. I use the word appear loosely, for in actuality I was concealed beneath the ranch-length mink coat tossed over me by my patroness to protect me and my only blue suit from a barrage of buttered breadsticks thrown *en masse* and pointedly in my direction by Mrs. Dali, who had either taken umbrage with the relaxed good time we were having or perhaps herself wanted to enhance the surrealistic company of the evening by some equally surrealistic behavior.

Thus began a period of magnificent excursions into an unimagined level of activity and companionship. My only dues besides staying alert and at my social best were to keep my shoes shined, hair well cut and groomed, and my one and only blue suit spotlessly clean and perfectly pressed. Fortunately, from the inception, my company was not only suitable but well liked, and before long I was taking this colossal leap in my social life in stride. More than all the opportunities I enjoyed, my greatest joy became the simple pleasure of the cordial friendship with the goddess on my arm.

A few months before the Debut, I arrived in New York to check some details and make some radio broadcasts. Liz had landed some Horowitz tickets and we nearly flew to Carnegie Hall to hear the master for our first time. I will never forget his Schumann Concerto Without Orchestra. This big and wrongly neglected work may well be Schumann's finest in the sonata form. His title characterizes Schumann's keen musicological and literary savvy, with 'Concerto' used in its purest meaning: concerted style or opposing musical forces, instead of indicating a soloist against an orchestra. Schumann's title not only describes the work but points to the essential character of its intended performance: a large-scale work of strong and dramatically opposing contrasts. In Horowitz's hands were the tempests of life and its struggles, mixed with the tender and all-too-vulnerable hopes of the heart and psyche, all undulating with fantastic rubato over a granite-like rhythmic framework, moving steadily along like the footsteps of fate itself. If you think I exaggerate, listen to the recording of this very performance.

Our combined euphoria was interrupted as we were headed off at the pass by the Town Hall manager and his wife, both smashed and insisting we join them for more drinks. We'd seen a lot of them both over the last year; they liked to claim me 'as their own.' However, little things here and there had not fallen on deaf ears, but were heard as small oddities and reminders that a little would be better than a lot. Naturally, I was grateful for what he'd done. The more we declined their generosities the more often and forcefully they were extended. We didn't know what was brewing, but as in all such situations in which one learns more than he would wish to know, the underlying truth is revealed by what is left unsaid.

Often Liz and I had managed polite exits from their rankling.

But today we were trapped behind cold food which got colder as he launched into a disquieting monologue about our acquaintanceship. Beginning with a ponderous listing of all he had done for me, it went on to 'how-one-never-gets-something-for-nothing,' and then sufficiently anesthetized, he fired into the heart, or shall we say, spleen of the matter. It seems I hadn't quite gotten the hint and if, bluntly put, I wanted to keep the debut, I would be expected to, shall I say, 'put out' for him. I sat dumbfounded. To this day there are probably tiny marks above my right knee where Liz's fingers clenched silent but painful meaning into my leg demanding, "Say nothing."

He complained that if I'd had a brain in my head, he wouldn't have had to spell it out so bluntly. On he went, suggesting once a week, perhaps an occasional trip. And for the jackpot, if I didn't take the hint seriously this weekend, he'd release the date to someone else. I managed to keep my mouth shut.

As I rose from my chair and tried to signal Liz that we do yet another quick exit, he blurted, "Ya know, Marco, when I tell people that we're presenting you at Town Hall, they say, 'Why?'"

I slumped back into my chair gathering my composure and said, "Well, first, that shows that I need the debut; and second, that if I had been doing what you suggest, no one would need to ask why. At least what you refer to as my stupidity for not catching on has resulted in the maintenance of your rather shaky reputation."

He threw his napkin on the table and snapped, "Then it's over. You can forget about the debut. It's done. Good-bye." His wife sat motionless and silent with a look of deep fatigue. She was there to do as she always did: pay the bill.

I got up again and put on my coat. It felt very good slipping it on—familiar, like home. I took Liz's free hand, the other wiping the tears running down her rosy cheeks.

"Alright," I said. "If that's how you feel, I guess that's how it is. I understand. OK. But call me tomorrow morning at ten, when you're sober. If you still feel this way, just say so."

I turned to walk away, then felt a stabbing pain in my chest. I froze and felt it pounding up my throat to my face, which felt as if it would pop. I turned back, placed my hands on the table and glared up at him. "But if you do cancel it, I promise here and now to not only take legal action, but to do whatever it takes to make sure people know the truth. You can forget me taking any 'high-road.' The gloves will come off. It's not even about me. It's about my folks, my teachers, all the people who have given all they could to me—who have never asked for anything except that I do my damnedest. I'll be damned if I'll let *you* do your damnedest now. If you do this, it is them you are cheating. And for that, you will pay."

I was filled with indignation, but somehow that night I slept soundly. I've fought some battles, some stupidly. But there is a point—a point like the one from which the Finns drove the Russians back—the point at which one demands respect in the clearest and most expedient terms. At that point, any price, any necessary loss simply makes one feel all the richer.

The next morning at ten the doorbell rang just as the phone rang. Liz was handed a dozen roses from our hosts of the previous night as I picked up the phone to profuse apologies and all the "Boy, was I drunk" nonsense imaginable.

With the Town Hall debut approaching, accumulated disappointments during my time in New York were beginning to spook me. Regardless of the contests I had won or the reviews I had received in Europe, I was growing increasingly concerned about being perceived as just a really good pianist but overlooked as a truly promising or unique artist. There had probably been more remarks about my unorthodox looks than genuine interest or notice of the individual style of my playing.

I hadn't complained about the nice review in Berlin's *Die Welt* which started with, "It is a rare stroke of luck when one hears a pianist with nothing to fault." Perhaps it was just a coming-of-age matter, a time when someone in my shoes looks within and asks, "Are they really going to hear what I'm doing? If not, is it their listening that is not good or is a part of my playing just not coming across or projecting to the listener?"

While not content to leave the issue up to the fates, three events would set me on a journey of musical re-discovery in the months just before my New York debut. They would also be remembered as important steps of an ongoing artistic self-evaluation.

One was that Horowitz recital—for if there were ever a pianist who sounded like no other, it was he. As if he used the piano to push out the sounds in his head, nothing was ever just played. Even a C Major scale, played slowly with a metronome, would have somehow sounded uniquely his. This recital gave me a kind of measuring stick with which I could ask, "How will this be heard in the second balcony of Carnegie Hall, where I sat for Horowitz?"

The second was a party in Boston that brought me back to all those long afternoons in the Portland library listening to the greats and my resulting understanding of what a performer's style really can be. While visiting a friend, he threw a party for a lot of his musical friends and other 'connoisseurs' of good music. At any such gathering, there's always the risk of encountering an 'expert.' In attendance at our gathering was a very assured Englishman, possessing no patience with any opinion other than his own. Frankly, he was a royal pain in the a—, but he did me a favor.

Over dinner he declared that once concert artists reach a certain level, they all begin to basically sound alike. He went on to insist that to tell one world-class pianist from another is really difficult, if not nearly impossible. Needless to say, I disagreed with him. At that point he suggested that if we had a few records of different pianists playing the same work, that beyond a lucky guess, I wouldn't be able to tell one from another. On cue, our host went to his huge record collection, saying that he could find six recordings of a short piece, and that he would like to see me try. Then he raised the stakes and bet Sir-Know-It-All a hundred dollars that I would name at least five out of six.

"You're on."

We took our desserts and coffee into the living room, where he found six recordings of Chopin's well-known E-flat Major Nocturne, each played by a different artist. In an unlikely moment of concern that I shouldn't make a complete fool of myself, the Englishman suggested that the names of the six artists be shared with me so that at least I'd have the benefit of choosing from some knowledge—a sort of multiple choice. However, I preferred to be given no knowledge of the identities.

Frankly, I hoped I might identify two or three correctly, but shortly, to my delight, I was naming one after another, sometimes, before the second measure. His lordship got really flustered. But not so surprising for me, having spent hundreds of hours as a teenager in my hometown library listening to absolutely everybody play absolutely everything.

Afterwards I wondered about how I knew so quickly and accurately each of the pianists. In most cases a particular element of playing—the balance, pedaling, even a feeling in the rhythm—provided the clue. In one or two others, my hint was the lack of some element combined with a good guess. I began to see how a systematic, objective reexamination of some fundamentals could have a strong impact on my playing. But should I jump into this kind of process so close to a big recital? Or should I try to remain comfortable and confident until the debut is over?

Long before, I had learned an important lesson that applied: one's standard of performance of a piece or a program should not, and cannot be simply maintained. It must consciously be improved or it will surely go downhill. Could this be true for the whole animal, the pianist himself? It seemed to me that one was really not distinct from the other; that is, the player or the program being played. So why split hairs? Knowing what I needed to do, and waiting even a day, regardless of schedule or risk, could spell disaster. It was a time when a valuable rule, hard learned, would be difficult to follow. I remained uneasy. On the very day my antipathy was making me nuts, I remembered an appointment to pick out a piano for the debut at Steinway Hall.

The effect on me from that visit to Steinway was rather like one of those young men in medieval times, who, seeking grace, knightly virtues, and aspiring to great deeds, must have felt the first time he stumbled onto King Arthur's castle, accepted an invitation to dinner, and was seated at the Round Table.

Located just down the street and across from Carnegie Hall, Steinway's somber but elegant decor is resplendent with large oil portraits accounting for most of the great pianists of the twentieth century. Rachmaninoff's riveting eyes peer down as Hofmann all but dares one to sit and play in one of the studio rooms—each resembling musical goldfish bowls with multi-paned, colonial-style windows for walls. Scattered everywhere are beautiful pianos of every size, color and style. One walks from room to room as if through a gallery of greatness.

The big surprise of that visit has been part of every single visit and phone call to this august realm ever since—the candid warmth with which I was treated. In the realm of the 'immortals,' I was being treated as if my portrait was in progress at that very minute. At a time when I was frustrated, flat broke, and often discouraged, I was touched at being received in the same manner as Ashkenazy or Van Cliburn surely had been.

At the far end of the building was a small complex of offices where, after a warm greeting from David Rubin, the director of the Concert Artists Division, I was given a guided tour of the rest of the building, including the famous basement where the concert pianos are stored. After trying several, I was informed that the particular piano they had hoped I would choose was out on a job. After repeated apologies, they urged me to consider using it sight unseen. I tried to decline as politely as I could, but when Mr. Rubin informed me that Gilels had it for several concerts over the next two weeks, that was good enough for me.

Ironically, in both New York and London, I performed or recorded just following a visit by this Russian giant. Relying on his flawless taste and expertise, I simply asked, "Which piano did Mr. Gilels select?" Besides relieving me of the time and expense of a trip to select a piano, it helped me to avoid developing quirky demands. Not only humbled by the connection, I felt it important to be able to handle myself on the piano that simply satisfied Steinway's specifications and the standards of a veteran.

When Horowitz made his triumphant Carnegie Hall return in the sixties, he specifically refrained from using his own Steinway, using one of the pianos from the Steinway fleet. Perhaps he felt it important that people knew his abilities were unconditionally all they had been. Oh yes, it was the concert grand Steinway Mr. Gilels had just used. Horowitz didn't bother to try it out either.

There is a lot to consider in playing a concert: rest, clothes, what to eat, lighting, placement of the piano, matters of tuning, voicing, action regulation, and even the chair or bench on which one will perspire heavily for the better part of two hours. Being specific and knowing what is needed is neither demanding nor temperamental. It is a sign of a true professional. But it is also the sign of a true professional to be able to give a fine performance under less than ideal circumstances.

The pressures on a young pianist coming under the scrutiny of press and public alike can, however, result in certain excesses. There's a story about Glenn Gould and his mania for sitting at just the right height. With the audience fully seated and lights lowered, a number of different chairs were ceremoniously brought out, left in front of the piano, and then taken away, only to be followed by another. After many attempts, one chair, with a thick telephone directory, was settled upon by the mysterious Mr. Gould, who remained offstage and invisible during this entire process. At long last, a delay in activity suggested that the pianist would appear and the concert could finally start. But in fact the stagehand once again returned to the platform. He walked to the chair, opened the phone book and tore out *one page*. Only at that point were things where they should be for the eccentric Canadian.

Returning upstairs, I was dumbfounded to be asked to sign on as a Steinway Artist. Over the years this honor has proven to be a great deal more than the considerable endorsement of one's abilities it suggests. But at the time, the compliment sent me walking home up Central Park West with a real spring in my step.

That evening I laid out a plan to critically examine my playing in general, along with efforts to steadily improve the debut program itself. During that difficult time, this fortunate decision helped me to turn away from worries over the success or failure of the debut and fully focus my energies on my own standards, where they belonged. I would look at balance; the meaning, length and shaping of a phrase; pedaling; the difference between playing in time and playing rhythmically; and at revealing form and shaping the dramatic line.

I'm not suggesting there aren't many other considerations to tackle and re-tackle with every piece. But over the years, especially through my opportunity to teach advanced players, I have discovered that a purely objective and rigorous re-examination of some fundamentals of playing and musicianship can have a tremendous impact, bringing forward and projecting the personality and uniqueness of an advanced performer.

After waiting and preparing for so long before a big concert, it seems suddenly to pounce upon you. The better part of a year had flown by, and now I was dressing for my debut in New York's Town Hall.

Again, my boyhood friend, Don Robertson, showed up to share his high-school pal's trauma and triumph. Mom and Liz had gone out to give me some precious peace at home. Liz had arranged the gift of a limousine to take me to the hall. Suddenly, the time to go had arrived. I called for Don's help with the mop of my hair which I'd forgotten all about. Only at times such as these does limp, fine, blond hair seem suddenly and valiantly to seize a will of its own. After minutes of combing and cursing, I grabbed in desperation for Liz's hairspray. When Don peeped in to investigate the hassle, I was furiously spraying and looking worse than ever. With special caution, Don told me I was using spray deodorant on my hair. Don threw a towel around my neck and, with both of us laughing and me on my knees under the bathtub faucet, washed all that goopy twenty-four-hour protection out of my hair.

My plan to arrive only a few minutes prior to the concert had failed to reach the hall manager, who had begun to contemplate the horrible possibility of a no show just about the time I briskly walked in. I had just enough time to check my tie, my fly, and to walk out.

At intermission, after a bravura knock on my dressing-room door and striding in with outstretched arms, Liz gathered me into an embrace of warm enthusiasm. Liz knew what my playing should be at its best, but she also wanted only the best for me. She was a good enough friend that if my effort might have been doing better, I surely would have heard why and how. Second only to solitary confinement, being in front of an audience can be the loneliest feeling in the entire world. When Liz left my room, due to her positive post-mortem of the first half of the recital, I realized that I was actually looking forward to playing the rest of the concert. One of the nicest parts of the evening was the stupendous party thrown by the hall director and his wife. Held at a posh, nearby restaurant in the Theater District, it remains in my memory as among one of the few after-concert affairs I've really enjoyed.

That night I learned that a performer's love for music is the key to overcoming fear, and is actually the indispensable ingredient needed to play his best. Instead of playing for our audience, rather we play to them, not simply making music as we play, but consciously demonstrating it as we guide the listener through every moment of the work.

A living dichotomy exists between thorough study and preparation on one hand, and the kind of risk-taking and enthusiasm indispensable to success before the public. This natural tension marks the distinction between a very good performance and one which can actually be perceived as having a life of its own: something which is played with an immediacy and sincerity, as if existing only in the moment of hearing, a performance bordering on recreation itself.

To accept being nervous, to practice in a way leaving nothing to chance, is to accept and understand that the natural excitement of public performance is the very thing which can enable one to actually transcend one's own abilities. It's a strange alchemy, but seen in this way, feelings of fear can actually become something else. The presence and supportive expectation of an audience can help you to find your courage, and in the flash of a moment, following your instincts can have wonderful results. In fact, only such high-pressure trials-by-fire provide the environment in which the true level of ability of a talented young artist can be revealed.

Mr. Mannheimer enjoyed relating a story about triumphing over fear. Attending the concert of one of his students at Wigmore Hall in London, during the performance he found himself being chastised by the companion with whom he sat. At intermission Mr. Mannheimer asked, "Why in heaven's name did you 'shush' me in that manner?"

The perplexed reply was, "Well Frank, perhaps you don't remember. But I heard you say in disbelief, 'He can't play that well.'"

During my time in New York City, my friendship with Samuel Barber became and remained my most precious relationship. In his presence, due to his self-effacing warmth and candor it was often difficult to be mindful of his genius and position in the world of music. His interest in me at that time, based on my professional status, was all but charitable. He chose to see the best in me and in my potential, taking me under his wing both musically and socially, teaching me a great deal, and honoring me with the level of regard in which he considered my opinions and youthful convictions.

About every two weeks, I would have dinner with him at his home on 5th Avenue, not far from the Metropolitan Museum of Art. During each visit, often into the wee hours, we would pour through the repertoire, from Bach to Barber (I still play a version of the Bach-Busoni Chaconne in the way we re created it during one of those splendid evenings). I brought to him loads of newer American works including many Sonatas. He had very high praise for those of Michael Hennigan (now published by Peters), and the big Donald Keats Sonata (published by Boosey and Hawkes), which he felt was darned near as good as his own, a landmark work.

He hoped that Keats would write a Piano Concerto. One evening, we had a fascinating talk on the subject. We basically agreed that the MacDowell d minor rests as the 'great' American Piano Concerto (I would say, second to Barber's). But we asked ourselves, "If one were to order up a piano concerto, what would be the ingredients one might ask for?" To this question we answered with three ideas:

1. A concerto needs to have the greatest possible dramatic extremes. It seems inherent in the form of piano vs. orchestra that the music itself should also reflect these extremes.
2. The work should be grateful to the solo instrument—that it has enough notes and sonority, as well as a high level of pianistic ease to serve as a successful vehicle for the pianist competing against a large orchestra in a big hall.
3. (And this we said out loud almost together), it should have great tunes.

Joe Whiteford was an organ builder for Aeolian Skinner, responsible for some magnificent instruments in this country including the great organ of the National Cathedral in Washington D.C. Born into the advantages of Ritten House Square in Philadelphia, he was a true connoisseur of piano playing and helped many fine young artists toward their careers.

Joe knew Barber from childhood. He told me a story about the awkward birth of Sam Barber's great Piano Concerto that is not so well known. It is known that Mr. Barber's 'block' in writing the final movement resulted in several pages a day being trickled to John Browning who was staying and practicing at Joe's place in Connecticut. With the ink barely dry, Mr. Browning received and mastered the last pages only days before the World Premiere performance in New York.

Early one morning a messenger delivered the entire middle movement. Over his first cup of coffee, Mr. Browning began reading the movement. Suddenly Joe rushed out from his bedroom with, "What the hell?" and without further comment grabbed the phone and pounded out the number to Sam Barber's 5th Avenue home. Still half asleep, as Barber picked up, Joe blurted out, "Sam, you've written 'Margie' in C-sharp minor." And sure enough, the theme was just too close to the old flapper era tune for comfort. In the finest tradition of creative collaboration, the two gentlemen, both in pajamas, made the necessary changes over the phone.

This particular tale was relayed to me by Joe. Mr. Barber was always modest, even self effacing about his efforts. When I sheepishly brought some possible changes for the Piano Concerto to him, he was not just tolerant but delighted, writing each in my full score with his signature. (I'm hoping G. Schirmer will keep their promise and include them in the next printing of the work. One was a modification of the tempo marking for the Finale—adding the words, "ma non troppo." Yes, one to a measure, but with each 8th note having 'muscle,' as he called it.)

During my middle twenties in New York City, although I fooled many while at the piano with playing sharply contrasting to the actual state of my personal development, away from the piano I was still a bit socially awkward. As both beneficiary and victim of my own zeal and hard work, there was no doubt that I had spent far too much time alone. However, the zeal of a young man passionately pursuing his life's ambition caught the eye of some famous and sometimes great artists. Guided by their collective compass, I found myself venturing toward a larger world. In this way the simple fact of living in New York City provided an invaluable opportunity for my personal and musical growth.

I found myself socializing with the likes of Anne Bancroft, Steven Sondheim, Gore Vidal and many others. Fascinating and exciting, rubbing shoulders with their success provided delicious vicarious departures from my yet impovrished and unrecognized life. Along with the huge success that I saw in these people was also their various histories in dealing with failure. From my years in New York, three stories about failure have remained in my memory. These I would like to share.

At the Broadway premier of his last play, all in attendance knew before the final curtain that Tennessee Williams would soon be facing the remains of an opening-night disaster. I was part of a group of about two-dozen young actors and musical artists invited to the performance and a dinner reception following. On the heels of a genuine flop, none of us were sure the playwright would even show up for the reception, so I was not only pleasantly surprised when Mr. Williams appeared, but genuinely stunned as he stood before us and presented a fatherly twenty-minute lecture about the need for artists to live in smaller towns, relatively free of the temptations and distractions of a place like New York City. He cited the productivity of his earlier years, living in the French Quarter in New Orleans. He spoke with a quiet sincerity which was not only generous in the extreme, but equally humbling coming from a man still reeling from the disaster occurring only moments before.

My last social meeting with Leonard Bernstein was over lunch in the Oak Room of the Plaza Hotel. Only a few weeks before he had conducted four long-awaited and much-anticipated performances with the Vienna Philharmonic Orchestra—perhaps the world's greatest, one which also chooses its own conductors democratically, a prize which had long eluded Bernstein.

Standard symphonic fare comprised the first three concerts which were heralded as no less than a musical marriage made in heaven by both the Viennese public and press. Some critical misgivings over the fourth collaboration would prove to be all but inevitable considering the work Bernstein chose to occupy the last position.

Having never conducted Strauss's opera *Die Rosenkavalier*, such a choice was dangerous. It is long, complex, difficult, subtle, and the best known and most beloved of all operas by the knowledgeable Viennese public. To have conducted a first performance of any work on such an occasion would have been to invite disaster. To offer a first attempt of *Rosenkavalier* was all but to guarantee it.

My story, however, is not about what happened as Bernstein conducted the Vienna Philharmonic, but how he characterized those concerts while speaking to me over lunch in the Oak Room by demanding that the critical misgivings over *Die Rosenkavalier* were completely the result of lingering and historical Viennese Anti-Semitism, of which he now considered himself the latest victim. Even pathological ambition cannot salvage the inevitable results from a lapse of basic common sense.

Mr. Bernstein's method of explaining away the Vienna lapse was not my only encounter with the oddities of his complicated, if brilliant, nature. Despite repeated efforts of a mutual friend, I never got the chance to play to him. Whatever he saw in me, my abilities as a pianist were not on the list. Nevertheless, I was always treated cordially during numerous meetings. But on Aaron Copland's ninetieth birthday, however, he outdid himself.

I had been asked by Mr. Barber to accompany the aging American composer, Aaron Copland, to a few parties to which he was obligated. I was honored to do so and did my best to be inconspicuous and attentive to his needs and frailty. When we arrived at the last party, held in a New York loft, Mr. Bernstein was 'holding court' in a far corner. Seated in a large chair, he was prophesying that the current Middle-East crisis would bring about no less than 'Armageddon,' as a group of intensely interested and equally well-groomed young men listened in motionless attention.

After greeting those in every other corner of the loft Mr. Copland begrudgingly said that we had to say "hello" and "good night" to Mr. Bernstein before we could go. When we arrived at Bernstein's group, Lenny couldn't rise to his feet to greet the man many believed to be America's preeminent composer. Following limp regards to Copland, when my unfortunate turn came, Bernstein began a long apology for never having heard me play. As he rambled on, I began to feel embarrassed to have my hat all but in my hand. As he said, "Goodnight," before I knew what was happening, he reached up, grabbing my head between two hands, pulled me forward and kissed me on the mouth—slipping me the tongue! I was speechless as Mr. Copland assisted me out of the room.

If Bernstein created his own reality or brashly acted on a momentary impulse, Barber brooded over issues, especially failure. In fact, it was an overwhelming fear of failure itself, which, having slowly grown over the years, shadowed his creative instincts and caused a relentless block to the compositional efforts of his later years. At its source were both the gargantuan successes of his early years as well as some personal pains, perhaps the worst being his rejection as a young man by the junior 'upstart,' Gian Carlo Menotti—a bitter and humiliating public jilting during the very apex of his career. In later years, along with the growing frailty of age, this nagging memory would jump the fence to join in raining havoc over the once radiant voice of American post-romanticism, slowly stifling Barber's confidence.

One of Mr. Barber's favorite piano works was the sensational, pyrotechnical "Scarbo," the third and final movement of Ravel's masterpiece, *Gaspard de la Nuit*. The three movements are musical settings of poems by Bertrand, the last being the spastic and terrifying activity on a gloomy evening of a demon-dwarf who flits about violently here and there in close proximity to the poet. At the climax Scarbo places his diminutive stature between the wall and the illumination of the poet's candle, with the result that the measure of his true stature is perverted beyond all reason to a shadow of towering terror. It is a potent symbol. To dazzling proportion by Ravel's musical and pianistic genius Scarbo conveys how a man can lose his grip on the true nature and size of a common threat, becoming irrationally terrified and unable to act.

In a real-life drama imitating art, this small marauding self-doubt from Barber's otherwise untroubled early manhood began to grow over the years to a stature resembling Scarbo's elongated shadow, whose puny source may have only been the unworthy public slight of a less worthy paramour. But over time, illuminated by the brightest musical beacon of the first half of the American Century, this became a towering shadow of the special breed of demons reserved only for the best among us, who,

Good Isn't Bad—Just Not Enough   89

by living both personal and artistic lives true to their own nature, risk the most—sometimes finding the greatest triumphs, but sometimes bedeviled by the special fears which prey on those among us who dare to reach beyond ordinary limits.

During my many evening visits amidst a gloomy alcoholic fog, whose predictable regularity would have marveled a railroad man, the hours after dinner most often brought Mr. Barber to a collision course with every conceivable antipathy. Nevertheless, despite occasional lapses into a bit of self-pity or even scorn, the lifelong habits of polite modesty and charm, forged from an advantaged and purposeful upbringing on Philadelphia's Rittenhouse Square, held such indulgences generally in check.

Frequently Mr. Barber recalled in near awe his early and heady days when a young genius must be all but on fire with artistic self-recognition. Barber's teenage arrival at Philadelphia's famed Curtis Institute was vividly shared with me in repeated evening retellings.

It was as if Mr. Barber took a nostalgic comfort that, although during those young days failure stubbornly shadowed, an inevitable and huge success would prove to be just around the corner. Now imprisoned in a relentless creative block, it seemed to me that by these frequent retellings Barber somehow hoped to rediscover the creative courage and vitality of those purely purposeful younger years.

When entering Curtis, young Samuel Barber declared singing as his primary musical study. But like all Curtis students of the day he was required to study piano secondarily as well. This demand was a demonstration of the underlying wisdom behind the Curtis legacy and its firm understanding that the prospect of any kind of professional musician without a basic mastery of keyboard was as inconceivable as that of a Harvard pre-law program tolerating general illiteracy. This policy created the happiest possible accident for the bumbling young Barber when he was assigned to the piano studio of Curtis's legendary tyrant lioness, Vengarova. Under her demanding gaze young Samuel was launched headlong into the Chopin Études, the Bach Preludes and Fugues and other cornerstones of the compositional and pianistic tradition.

This was no less than a trial by fire for Barber, who diligently forged ahead doing the best he could, practicing the piano to hours of slavish excess. In all of our chats he never mentioned his study of voice nor composition at Curtis. The study was all there, as would be well evidenced by the treasured variety of works of his legacy. But, the unique and privileged contact to Vengarova provided an unlikely advantage to Barber's arsenal of natural melodic gifts, for no other American composer since MacDowell has approached Barber's deft command of the intricate technical secrets generally known only to the high priests of pianist-composers like Chopin and Liszt. Despite a small output, this knowledge, acquired under Vengarova, would play the pivotal role in propelling Barber's Piano Sonata and later, the Piano Concerto to positions of absolute prominence in those idioms of American music.

At the death of Franklin D. Roosevelt, an orchestral transcription of the slow movement of Barber's String Quartet, popularly called "Adagio for Strings," would become the signature song of mourning for an entire nation. Its countless broadcasts over countless radio stations in countless cities and towns brought to young Barber a level of popular fame and public recognition that, as he often expressed to me, might have been more than he wanted. A very real conflict existed in the daily comings and goings of a young man of genteel and sensitive demeanor suddenly thrust headlong into the riveting and constant speculation of public scrutiny.

In his late years the growing demon resulting from excessive early fame in sharp contrast to at least one publicly embarrassing personal debacle may have created in Barber a genuine professional timidity contrasting sharply with his huge artistic gifts.

I noticed another conflict in Barber's own reflections of his opera *Cleopatra*—that is, his many mentions of that work to which he never referred by name—quietly snarled out rather as, "MY DISASTER." Resembling the presence of an unwelcome relative, his unhappy memory of the critical debacle of his opera's opening made Barber neither unable to live with it nor to deny its existence.

In time Cleopatra's early difficulty may prove to have been only a shaky start to an enormously promising work. Sometimes works of such size and complexity need a bit of loving care, seasoning and even tailoring in order to find their true worth. Barber may have allowed himself to be undone and rushed to a hurtful acquiescence of the critics' and ever-present naysayers' negative judgment.

Now, years after Barber's death and living on independently from the hands of its creator, Cleopatra seems a potential masterpiece in search of a compositional spirit kindred to Barber's, but free of the personal foibles behind abandoning his 'child.' Unlike Dumbo's mother who railed against the snickering of onlookers over her child's ears, Barber's mantra of "My Disaster" carried with it the evidence of his only true failure: his unwillingness or inability to stand by his creation.

Barber's true genius will shine on in *Cleopatra*, enduring not only its less than luminous start but the lapse represented by Barber's neglect. Samuel Barber's compositional greatness is such that, even after his own passing, *Cleopatra* may very well make its own way forward in the world.

When I entered Oberlin, I saw many pianists of conspicuous talent all around. During my four years, there seemed a natural process in which some distinguished themselves more than others. I learned that talent played a part in that process, but not the most important one. Neither did advantaged prior training or even the relative abilities of Oberlin's principal teachers in determining the outcome.

Despite our differences and various histories of study, entering the environment peculiar to a conservatory itself presented an undeniable common denominator to be shared by all as we faced a new level and number of pressures, expectations and even personal demons. Now there were as many ways of imagined failure as there were students themselves, and it would be the way in which each student learned or failed to learn to deal with his own issues in fear of failure which ultimately determined the extent of long-term development.

Genuine talent and personal courage began to appear as intimately intertwined, with the key to their healthy union being found ultimately in the quality of attitude behind each day's work. Those able to reaffirm and build upon a strong connection to a simple, basic childhood love of music found the key not only to genuine and conspicuous improvement, but also to the means by which a plethora of demons inhabiting the demanding realm of high-level, classical-piano study could be held in check all along the way to, and including, the minefields of public performance and competitive critical comparison.

Having left school a few years behind, during the period approaching my debut at Town Hall, I began to learn about not only dealing with fear and pressure but the indispensable role of each in achieving playing even beyond one's best. Efforts to develop a more recognizable musical signature in my playing by pursuing some areas of objective scrutiny had yielded a thoroughly subjective improvement, marking the beginning of a process which continues to this day.

In the week following my New York debut, a careless oversight resulted in a fortunate revisiting of the relationship between attitude in daily work and its impact on fear and the ultimate quality of my playing. Just days after Town Hall, I was scheduled to play a recital in Shreveport. Don and I had decided to meet in New Orleans the next morning for several days of much needed rest and relaxation. En route to New Orleans the true scale of pressure and stress under which I had been anticipating the debut finally became clear as a glance at my calendar lowered the boom on me. I had overlooked an engagement for a pair of concerts with the Richmond Symphony on which I would play the Beethoven 1st Piano Concerto. Chagrin almost instantly became panic as it dawned on me that, with only seven days to the first rehearsal, it just also happened to be a work that I didn't know.

Don knew what was at stake and deftly redirected my embarrassed apologies toward efforts to secure a place for what would be six days of grueling practice. To my rescue came Phillip Werlein, owner of the big Steinway dealership in New Orleans, who graciously offered a fine Steinway in the living-room at his home just a short trolley ride from the French Quarter. I practiced two three-hour sessions every day, with a long break for lunch and a walk or a bit of 'R-&-R,' only meeting Don for dinner and an evening suitably short for a pianist in training and under the gun.

As I began my work I was in too much of a dither to have imagined the value of my introduction to Mrs. Werlein. My first notion of her presence was the delicate scent of her perfume as she walked toward me like a gentle breeze through lace curtains. At first glance I saw not only a face disfigured by the surgical solution to a terrible cancer of the lower jaw, but also the face of a still beautiful, if slightly older woman. She spoke with the mellifluous Southern cadence of a history and role in a long tradition devoted to and reflective of the beautiful in life. Beyond a feeling of something in common, we were, as the Southern quip suggests, 'like a pair of cold chickens to a hot brick,' and spontaneously we joined in what would be a week-long and heartfelt dialogue—one which she reinvigorated at each break of my practice ordeal.

From the pressure of the schedule under which I labored, I was pursuing a practice strategy of setting aside loftier artistic considerations in favor of first securing fundamental memory and technical issues. Amidst a hurricane of concentrated energy, Mrs. Werlein would drift into the room and quietly admonish me with, "Mark, you must always play with love."

I tried to explain my strategy and my concerns of making sure in the limited time I had of securing some basic issues. But to this she responded, "Mark, darling, I understand. But always play with love. No matter what—play with love."

Blinded by pressure, I didn't yet understand, politely reiterating my strategy. But in short order my hostess had understood that even in the name of safety, my attempt to marry my fears in some kind of happy arrangement to what I thought to be a positive agenda was in fact an exercise in futility. She relentlessly, but kindly, insisted that I was not only condemning the product to one representing less than my best, but was actually sowing the seeds of the very disaster I was working so hard to avert.

Again she said, "Mark honey, play with love. Always play with love."

Over those days her mantra changed not one syllable, and I found my arguments giving way to a larger, deeper sense of what she seemed to be saying. From our conversations I began to understand that she'd sensed in me the rustlings of an anger or even cynicism, which can grow from the constant rejection or even neglect a young artist relentlessly faces. She understood that while often frustrated and still short of one's goals, it is all too easy to be seduced by an agenda reflective of fears. In the light of her history as a performing pianist and her personal wisdom she had learned that there was only one way forward under any and all circumstances, and that even the reliability of memory and technical security is dependent upon a work attitude reflective of the simple joy and enthusiastic discovery of making music.

At the end of the week I arrived in Richmond, where I received a standing ovation for my first performance. The next morning I was greeted by a review that was so good I found myself rushing to finish breakfast and practice before the day's matinee performance. I was determined to live up to the critic's gushing. The reaction all around was a strong piece of encouragement suggesting that my playing was now better projected and thus perceived by my listeners.

This period would prove to be a turning point in my playing. Although I didn't feel particularly different while I played, there was no doubt that there was a difference in what people were hearing. I had begun to separate myself artistically from the pressures and foibles of a professional musical career, re-igniting a quality of simple and genuine musicality reflective of the basic love of music and joy of playing that I had felt since childhood. This improvement brought me full circle to the very threshold of the goals for which I had long yearned. Ironically, the complexities, pressures and difficulties encountered in the pursuit of any career can prey upon and undermine the very qualities upon which success depends. No matter what, even when frustrated, disappointed, angry, and especially when afraid, one must always, *always* "play with love."

Management and the Age of the Gimmick

As a little boy, long before I even starting taking piano lessons, I was well used to the company of others endowed with large musical gifts. My sister Martha, three years older than I, possessed a fine childhood playing ability and showed the kind of general promise that could have developed in any of a number of musical directions. In this kind of company, I was therefore not uncomfortable exhibiting my early delight for music by a willingness to play in the company of someone well along. Perhaps more importantly, I was learning not to feel threatened, nor in any way put down by my unaccomplished state. Instead I was fully absorbed by the magic of the musical world I was beginning to encounter.

In my own little world of blissful ignorance, prior to any lessons or formal training, I was a prisoner of the white keys—merrily using the piano as my personal sound-effects machine for 'blood-and-guts,' child-sized dramas, made up as I went along. Already, playing the piano was as natural as falling off a log, or in my case, climbing up onto the bench with the company of my pink elephant, in the smiling and tolerant gaze of parents or other onlookers. This penchant for storytelling became the essence of making music for me but was not necessarily limited to association with a piano. In short order the natural consequence of events would make "show and tell" my very favorite part of the school day when I entered kindergarten.

During my high school years, several first-rate talents a year or two older than I, and two fabulous boys my same age, studied with another teacher in town. When I lost a local contest to one of these fellows, any letdown or disappointment usually evaporated in the car about halfway home as I began to think about the next piece I wanted to play. My resilience at times in which another youngster might have been crushed or disappointed was the natural reaction to my early childhood years surrounded by abilities larger than my own. Like anyone I wanted to prevail, but was fortunate not to see my success and failure as at the center of the universe. I believe this attitude of simple personal devotion to something I viewed as ultimately greater and more important than myself carried me through dark periods, and even beyond the supposed limits of my natural abilities. Years later it would actually rescue me from the biggest challenges of my life.

When I entered John Perry's class at the Oberlin Conservatory, I was one of four talented freshman boys, any one of whom a teacher in his position would have coveted. Besides our view of each other's gifts, we were also only freshman and had all the upper classmen as well with whom to contend. With my history, however, rather than feeling threatened, I felt more excited than ever, simply rolling up my sleeves and working harder. By the time I arrived in New York this innate love of music and a long-forged willingness to work hard, combined with an unusual ability to happily take and process criticism and learn from nearly everyone I encountered, served me well.

Even during my last year at Oberlin and my time as a graduate student at Eastman, I was playing quite a few concerts around the country. My victories in several competitions had served to begin a promising reputation, and by the time I arrived in New York I had no substantial reason to doubt that I was generally on the right track toward a career. However, precisely at the time of my arrival in New York I became suspicious that the very best in my playing didn't seem to matter much to the professional musical community that haunted the classical scene. As a matter of fact, I soon began to think that the whole issue of my abilities as a performing pianist, or my clear promise as a successful performer and future concert artist, were of little importance.

Now in my mid-twenties, during the mid-1970s I was about to learn that the classical music business in New York was itself going through enormous contortions, creating equally enormous difficulties for anyone in my position. It seemed to me that the management business was largely populated by a number of very nervous men and a few even more nervous women, most of whom mistrusted and disliked each other, and who participated in a kind of ongoing cold-war of gossip, lawsuits, and endless recriminations. On the surface, all this was put forward as to be in the interests of various artists. But none of it ever did the artists any good, and often the artists, desperate to exit a relationship with a manager who was finding them little work and costing them a fortune, were actually the targets of the lawsuits.

It seemed as if many managers were suffering a kind of shell-shock from the Van Cliburn phenomenon of the late fifties with the enormous press, public adoration, and ticker-tape parades—all wrapped up with boyish all-American good looks, indisputable wit and charm, and the onstage pedigree of a truly fine and noble artist. Although Van's sudden public acclaim was in fact not the overnight surprise it may have seemed, the degree of his fame was perhaps unlike anything the classical music business had ever seen. In the darkest days of Cold War tensions, with Khrushchev staring down Kennedy and pounding his shoe on a United Nations table, Van's wonderful win of the first Tchaikovsky International Piano Competition in Moscow thrust his image onto front pages, early television and even the news reels in movie houses across the country.

Many of my friends felt that the problem with New York management in those days was that, without admitting so, most managers were secretly looking for their very own Van Cliburn and a quick ticket to big success. As a result, the situation for a new talent to be seen or heard on his own terms and promise was more than difficult.

Long before the Second World War, the young impresario Sol Hurok sensed a special quality in the hot-blooded and poetic Arthur Rubenstein, even when his playing may have been prone to messiness, with press and public reactions in America and abroad more than uneven. But Hurok trusted his instincts, and he fought loyally at Rubenstein's side for many years to finally see the artist's promise blossom into a legendary stature. This kind of artist/manager equation depended on ingredients of keen artistic instinct, a loving, nurturing nature, and an uncommon level of steadfastness, personal ethics, and downright loyalty, even during times when the artist himself may have been losing his way or his faith in the eventual outcome.

Hurok and a man by the name of Arthur Judson were two from that period of management in New York City who set examples of artistic judgment, public intuition, loyalty and ethical behavior which had all but vanished by the time of my arrival. By then, the sense of partnership between manager and artist had deteriorated badly to one resembling patron and parasite—but which was which?

Now managements were promoting artists on the basis of a number of reasons other than their own positive opinion about the artists' playing and potential for public success. As a result the managers' credibility with buyers around the country who had relied on their judgment and knowledge for so many years began to erode. This is one of the reasons competitions became so important. Managers were often selling competitions more enthusiastically than the young artists who had won them.

Now, sadly, when a manager said, "I love his playing, so will you," no longer could a long—disillusioned buyer be persuaded. Because managers had stopped promoting artists they themselves loved, in favor of those they simply thought would sell, they had in turn sold out their own reputations, indispensable to their part of a successful equation. The age of the gimmick had arrived. In my opinion, with a few lucky exceptions, this betrayal of trust has resulted in far too many of our very finest and most captivating performing artists of classical music living all but obscure public lives.

A violinist friend of mine, who during this period lived in New York City and played second stand, first violins in the famed NBC Orchestra under the great Arturo Toscanini, had his own feelings about music management. He felt that another problem was due to the change in motivation behind those choosing careers in artist management. Before, it had often been someone who we might casually describe as a bit of a 'frustrated artist,' determined to find a niche in the music business aside greatness, if not center-stage. Now, former salesmen and other merchandisers began filling the slots vacated by the members of the 'old code' such as Hurok and Judson. Lacking the kind of visceral involvement in the art itself, and thereby having less than the required intimate artistic and personal relationship, they were unwilling or unaware of their role as a true artistic partner in creating a long-term performance career.

Another, and perhaps the most devastating, reason for career difficulty during this period was rooted in national politics and social change. For decades, the recital series on college and university campuses had represented the largest single playing field for both established artists and eager newcomers. With the cultural upheaval of the 60s and early 70s, this nationwide resource was nearly decimated as vast numbers of these recital series were put in the hands of student committees and replaced by rock concerts. From my point of view, the inmates were running the asylum. Not that rock concerts hadn't existed before, but it seemed now that any and all things with an aura of tradition were seen as suspect and even defined as 'counter-revolutionary' by some of the louder, more militant factions. In a nationwide frenzy, often lacking common sense and good leadership on both sides, classical music was thrown into a condition of chaos where once a fertile field had existed.

Due to these and other reasons, long careers were suddenly threatened to extinction. Relations between artists and managers were strained to the limit, with grim prospects of success for newcomers. In many firms, recently signed young artists and new prospects were unceremoniously dropped with little or no notice. This was the case when the old Hurok office was taken over from within and renamed ICM. I know, because I was awaiting an appointment to visit the president's office and sign a contract resting in the top drawer of his desk. In that moment, my years of effort in New York came to nothing as former President Roger Hall stepped down, replaced by Shelly Gold, and I learned that my years of work and hope were dashed.

In an atmosphere resembling the politics of a ten-bed orphanage with eleven orphans, concert careers routinely burned shorter than ever before. It became begrudgingly acceptable to promising young artists, following a victory in an important competition, to hope for perhaps two or three years of playing followed by a polite departure to a good university position. In this situation the cream rarely rose to the top and almost never stayed there.

In hindsight, having now witnessed for myself these troubling changes in my profession, my bizarre first encounter with music management seemed to make a certain peculiar kind of sense. When I first arrived in

New York shortly after my recitals in Europe, Mr. Mannheimer suggested that a personal recommendation from an important and active artist might be helpful in securing the interest of a well-established New York management. His hope was that I could begin slowly, growing steadily over time, so that the level and longevity of a career would be, as Mr. Mannheimer put it, "a sure thing."

During winter term of my last year at Oberlin, when I had visited Mr. Mannheimer in London, he arranged for me to play to the great English pianist Clifford Curzon, who expressed not only his approval of my playing but his willingness to open a professional door at the appropriate time. Now with that in mind, Mr. Mannheimer contacted Curzon who wrote a wonderful letter in my behalf to the gentleman who had just inherited the distinguished Arthur Judson firm in New York, longtime managers of Curzon and other fine pianists.

When I got a call from the new president inviting me to play to him, I was very excited, to say the least. My audition would take place on no less than centerstage of Carnegie Hall, due to the kindness of Hall Manager Stu Warcow. I had met Mr. Warcow on a New York trip during my graduate study at Eastman, and it might have been my boyish enthusiasm that had put him on my side.

You can't imagine how difficult it can be to arrange an hour of time under reasonable conditions with a reasonably good instrument for an audition in New York City. To have been able to say, "I believe I can arrange an hour at Carnegie Hall," was wonderful. Besides the panache of being heard on the platform of America's most renowned hall, there was the simple convenience of being right in the middle of "Managers Row" on 57th Street.

The audition went off well, and I was invited to come across the street to the Arthur Judson offices for a chat. With little preamble, he began, "I think you might be the best young American pianist I've heard since 'Willie' Kapell." I was dumbfounded, but after squeaking out a thank you, I sat silently as he began looking anxiously around the room, as if following a meandering insect.

"You look all wrong... blond, blue eyes... you look like a damned surfer, not a pianist. How the hell would I ever market you? You don't fit at all. Even the repertoire on your list is all wrong. Look at all these huge German works, Schubert Sonatas, Beethoven's "Hammerklavier," the Brahms F-minor Sonata, Bach Partitas...You're really out of the mainstream, kid."

At that point I meekly asked if that in itself couldn't be a selling point. "Couldn't the things you call different be positive? After all, everybody says they're always looking for something different...."

Rubbing his chin, he muttered, "Yes, maybe.... The playing's definitely there; the reviews are there; you've got the competitions; I'll bet you're good with an audience..." And he broke off suddenly, looking up as if in surprise. "Have you ever heard of a retainer, kid?"

Startled, I replied, "A retainer?"

"You heard me." Now leaning forward and scrutinizing me carefully, he said, "A retainer of, say, $10,000. Could you raise it? Do you have it?"

I explained that I might be able to approach a group of friends to raise the money if I could give them an understanding of the expenses against which the retainer would be placed, i.e. publicity, phone calls, office expenses, perhaps even some managers' commissions paid at the signing of a contract if necessary...

With disbelief coming across my face, he began to make it clear that these funds would not defer any expenses—all of that would be in addition. I mentally pinched myself and half-jokingly inquired if he meant that I should simply give him $10,000. To that, he simply and solemnly nodded.

As I began to feel the entire affair dissolving beneath my feet, I told him that I could never ask my friends for what he proposed. Furthermore, regardless of what he might have said about my playing, and despite my general ignorance as a newcomer, I felt that if a manager needed to be paid or bribed to take on a new pianist, it simply would never work, needing rather to believe not only in my potential, but in his own abilities. I stiffly rose from my chair, chagrinned over Mr. Curzon's wonderful recommendation being dashed on the rocks with such shady burlesque hokum. Not only disappointing to me, I was beginning to anguish over the letter that I would have to write to Mr. Curzon.

As I reached for my coat, I said, "So you're telling me, this $10,000 would basically go about here," and I patted my hip pocket.

The reply was, "I suppose you could say that."

"Well then, I think we have nothing else to discuss."

It became painfully obvious over the next couple of years that regardless of my abilities and my success with both critics and the public, this blond, blue-eyed kid from Portland, Oregon, was just not what the New York managers were looking for. My chance would have to come another way. I've been asked several times why I didn't become discouraged and quit. Well, I suppose if my problems with managers had had much to do with my abilities as a performing artist, I might have. But it seemed as one disappointment followed another, the likes of Van Cliburn, Vladimir Ashkenazy, Leon Fleischer, Sergio Commissiona, and Sir Georg Solti urged me to keep going.

It would be a quirk of fate which drove me to find my own niche as a touring soloist. My mother was diagnosed with a serious abdominal cancer and an uncertain future. Without hesitation I closed my apartment in New York and returned to my parents' home in Portland. Fortunately a single surgery did the trick, and before long she was well on the mend. And so, to my great and everlasting surprise, would be my floundering career.

Yanked out of New York, I struck up a relationship with a new manager just in the process of putting a stable of new young artists together. With his office in New York City and me based again at home in Portland, I began to travel at every opportunity from city to city, meeting and playing to the local conductor or orchestra manager. If I was booked in the Midwest, I would stop at one or two places going and coming. Besides the hearings for myself, I was now being evaluated in the first person—on my own merits as a young artist. Before too long, engagements started being offered.

In a way, I had become my own road man. I was sometimes criticized for being overly aggressive. Probably true. But the fact was either this or no career at all. I worked like a dog but made a lot of friends. My record of re-engagements in many cities was unusually good since many of the places considered me somewhat of their own discovery.

Over time this process took me first to Sergio Commissiona, conductor of the Baltimore and Houston orchestras, and then eventually to the Chicago Symphony, Sir Georg Solti, and my passport to playing all over the world. Down the line better management would fall into place for me as a natural result of the success of my own endeavors. Perhaps this is not the way I wished it had happened or it even should have happened, but this was the way it did happen, and I am grateful for the support of family, friends, and fans, via my own peculiar route which led to my goal.

While other young artists dealt with these same issues of management, there was another issue I would never have anticipated. During my college years I'd struck up a close friendship with the family of one of my schoolmates. They were of Jewish background and lived in a fine big home in Larchmount, about forty-five minutes north of New York City. My next-door neighbor at the time was a man named Harry Beall. He was the head of fund-raising for the United Jewish Appeal, and a good friend.

During one of the short but savage wars which Israel fought during those years, I received an urgent evening phone call from my Larchmount friends asking me if I could perform an appropriate piece the next afternoon for about one hundred guests who were coming to make contributions for the Israeli war effort. I was up all night practicing Beethoven's majestic and angry "Appassionata" Sonata. The next day, after an afternoon of spirited talk and much weeping, I performed this mighty work. When I finished, the place went up in shouts that I will never forget. As I was ushered to the kitchen and told that nearly a quarter of a million dollars had been raised, I felt a sense of deep pride in being a small part of the day's history.

As I slumped over a sandwich in the kitchen, a middle-aged man came in, introduced himself, and told me that he had been in the music business for over thirty-five years. With that he said, "You are the finest young American pianist I've heard since 'Willie' Kapell. It's a shame you're not Jewish; I could probably do something for you…" I was so flabbergasted that I don't remember much more than my angry hostess hurriedly pushing him from the room.

Returning to my apartment, I got a knock on the door from my neighbor, who had received a phone call from my hostess outlining the success of the fund-raising efforts as well as her concerns over the matter in the kitchen. He asked me if I could freshen up and come over to his apartment. When I tried to bow out gracefully due to fatigue, he insisted, saying it would be very important to come, even if just for a moment. When I arrived he took me by the arm through the crowded rooms and introduced me to Golda Meir. She took me up in both of her hands, kissing me warmly on the forehead and thanking me for the part I had played in the afternoon's efforts. With a sigh, she then told me that she had heard about the comment made in the kitchen and asked me to understand that her people were not only complicated but also at a very complicated time in their history.

Needless to say, the meeting was an unforgettable experience. Although her gracious efforts more than laid aside any wounded feeling I might have had earlier that day, and despite the fact that my Jewish friends were outraged by this attitude, from time to time I would encounter others in the music business that thought as this gentleman had—seeing no wrong in it—simply business as usual—a fact of life. I learned never to draw attention to this episode nor others like it and especially never to complain about it, because to do so was to be instantly labeled an anti-Semite by the very people who practiced this kind of reverse prejudice.

Myths and Legends: The Show Must Go On!

During these years of chasing an uncertain career and encountering troubling oddities of the music business and of human nature, often only the condition of my playing seemed in my own hands. Therefore, it was with a near vengeance that I relentlessly worked to improve, becoming almost too tough on myself, sometimes able only to think of the flaws of a performance that might have just received a standing ovation. However, after a little time and a bit more success I grew more relaxed and philosophical about little shortcomings. Of help also were some stories that came my way about other pianists.

It's not unusual for a young pianist to believe that some of the giants like Rubenstein, Rachmaninoff, Cortot, Gieseking, and Schnabel had few if any limitations to their abilities. It's good to remember, however, that they worked like slaves, encountering their own difficulties.

Mrs. Genhart once told me about the last time she heard Busoni play the complete Chopin Etudes. As she said, "He had lost his nerve and was drinking heavily, regularly, even before recitals." She described the first Etude as "almost unrecognizable," the second was still a mess but perhaps a little better, but through the third and by the fourth, his playing somehow had returned to the level of its legendary stature; in fact, even better than in previous years.

Mrs. Genhart told me about this when I visited her in Zurich prior to my first European recital tour. Only a few weeks before, she heard Pollini perform the complete Etudes, having just recorded them magnificently for Deutsche Gramaphone. With the exception of some of the slower, more melodic studies, she said that Pollini's was the best performance of this landmark she had heard since Busoni himself.

A couple of weeks later when I was in Hamburg, I visited the Steinway factory and got into a talk with the artist representative who recently had been a part of the recording sessions in which Pollini had put down the Etudes for his staggering recording. Following his praise of the final product, he revealed that the project was among the most difficult in which he'd ever been a part. Evidently, Pollini suffered terribly with days of frustration, shed many tears, and on more than one occasion, but for the faith and the support of the crew and his associates, the project was nearly abandoned altogether.

Great achievements require great efforts. Genuine suffering can be the fire which forges mighty accomplishments. For one who strives for excellence, this anguish has meaning: it becomes an ally. Rachmaninoff said, "Drudgery is part of being an artist."

When Dinu Lipatti was asked to play the 'Emperor' Concerto, he told the concert organization that he would need five years to have it ready to his standards. In contrast, Walter Gieseking learned the huge Rachmaninoff Third while on tour in a matter of a few weeks. He gave it a 'run-through' in New Jersey, and about a week later played it in Carnegie Hall with Rachmaninoff in the audience, who afterwards declared Gieseking the finest living exponent of his music.

My friend Dean Elder, who studied with Gieseking, once asked this most gifted of all pianists why he no longer performed the Schumann Toccata in public, particularly since he used to open programs with it as a young man. Gieseking's reply was that it had become a "bit of a strain." That was all. On another occasion, Dean asked him why he had never performed the Chopin B minor Sonata. Although Gieseking was not known in this country for his Chopin performances, those few that we have on record are ravishing, and he played a great deal of it in Europe, especially during his younger years. But Gieseking's reply was that he had once heard Cortot play the work so well that he just never picked it up.

Rachmaninoff once was sitting with Gieseking at a Carnegie Hall recital of Josef Hofmann. At the end of the Chopin B minor Sonata, Rachmaninoff's head slumped downward as Gieseking heard him mutter, "Well, there goes another piece out of my repertoire."

When Rachmaninoff came to this country, he went, like all Russian pianists new on the scene, to see Godowsky. After some polite conversation, the already renowned Rachmaninoff began to complain that he was committed to a very big recital tour the very next season. To this Godowsky exclaimed, "You're complaining?" Rachmaninoff explained that he did not have a real recital program in his repertoire, and that most of his solo playing was restricted to his own works and some works of Scriabin. Half-dazed by this revelation, Godowsky patiently sat down and began to outline the kind of process that might be expected: first maybe some Scarlatti or Bach, then a nice Mozart or Beethoven Sonata, followed by some Debussy and something brilliant before intermission; after, perhaps some of his own works would be nice, a contrasting work, and then a Liszt group ending with a Rhapsody or Mephisto Waltz, or the Polonaise and the like. He then went to his library and took out a bunch of scores, heaping them into Rachmaninoff's arms and as he said goodbye, made a few suggestions on the lines of "not too much pedal or rubato in the Scarlatti, Bach, and Mozart," and so on.

Young Vladamir Horowitz spent quite a lot of time on the Chopin B minor Sonata but never performed it publicly. There's a story that I'm not absolutely sure is true, but I like nevertheless. A brash young reporter for the New York Times managed to arrange an afternoon interview with the elusive Horowitz during which he finally asked the master why he had never performed the Chopin B minor Sonata. Over and over the cunning Horowitz dodged the question, perhaps for good reason. But as the reporter repeated the question, demanding an answer, finally Horowitz blew his top, exploding, "First movement—too long; second movement—too short; third movement—too long again; fourth movement—too damned difficult!"

John Browning's mother told me that her son had been a bit anxious about the last round of the Queen Elizabeth Competition in which one learned a commissioned work in one week and performed it along with a concerto in the finals. To make sure he could, he tackled the difficult Barber Sonata in a week. Some years later, Mr. Browning was invited to make a recording of the 2nd and 3rd Prokofiev Concerti. He had only about a week to prepare them and he did not know the 2nd. It's a big piece, but he did it. This falls under the category of something in which I firmly believe: "Preparation is the key to opportunity" (Frank Mannheimer).

I've often said that the composer does not exist without the performer. Even a composer of great acclaim must face the uncertainty of having his best efforts exhibited in the hands of others. Mr. Barber told me about taking the train to Long Island a week or two before Horowitz was to give the world premiere of Barber's fabulous Piano Sonata in Carnegie Hall. Mr. Barber sat stunned as Horowitz began to play a work which was almost unrecognizable. He heard his Sonata running through what was being played, but it seemed to bear little or no resemblance to the work as written—almost like all the pages of the work had been dropped on the floor, picked up randomly and played.

At the concert's conclusion Mr. Barber went backstage, gathering his courage, and meekly asked Horowitz if what he had heard was altogether according to the score. Horowitz nonchalantly replied that he liked to play around with big works, as if recomposing them, but that when Mr. Barber heard it the next time in Carnegie Hall it would be absolutely faithful to the score—and in fact, it was.

Another uneasy meeting of composer and performer happened while I was a student at Oberlin and was put upon to perform Milton Babbit's nasty, serial-type work, "Partitions". Every note had a different dynamic marking, ranging from pppp to the opposite extreme. The rhythms were inconceivable as well, with seven against thirteen against whatever, with rests thrown in, and in groups starting at different places . . . you name it. Impressive on the page and difficult to play, it lacked any discernible large form, probably because of its own lack of efficiency. Relentless complexities and dissonance even made it monotonous.

With only two weeks to prepare, on the day before the performance, I was told that Babbit was insistent upon hearing me play the piece. I was terrified. Not only did I hate his piece, but I'd Xeroxed it and completely redone every detail, changing the bar lines, altering dynamics and rhythms, trying for some idea of a line.

When I entered the studio to play for the composer, I barely stopped to shake his hand, going right by to the second piano, that is, as far away as possible from where he sat with the score in his lap. When I finished, the silence was terrifying. He shook his head, flipping pages back and forth as he looked almost in disbelief. Then, slowly, he peered up over his glasses and solemnly said, "That was the most perfect rendition of my work I've ever heard."

———◆———

When one is in his early twenties and on fire, it's natural to explore and expand one's limits in tackling difficult works. But it can nearly drive one crazy. Years can be spent, sometimes ending in bitter frustration, sometimes triumph. Works like Beethoven's "Hammerklavier" Sonata were written with little or no concern about their playability. There are show pieces that sound hard and are hard: the Schumann Toccata, Balakirev's "Islamey," "Scarbo" from Ravel's "Gaspard de la Nuit." These and others contain, as part of their musical effect, obvious and treacherous difficulty.

A work containing big difficulties all around is the wonderful "Mephisto Waltz" by Liszt. The day before my first performance of it, during the long walk to the Oberlin Conservatory, I was caught in a heavy downpour. Eager to practice for the next evening, I forged through the torrential rain and arrived soaked. What did I care? I was young and strong. The rest of the day seemed normal enough. I even slept soundly, an uncommon occurrence the night before a performance. But I awakened the following morning horrified to find myself with a high fever and aches and pains all over. "What curse was this?" I thought, forgetting all about my stupidity of practicing soaked to the skin.

I spent most of the afternoon in bed and ate a light dinner alone, just in time to dress and warm-up for the performance. Completely exhausted, sick, and a little crazy, I walked on stage to face my adversary. The place was packed. I prayed to survive Liszt's minefield and began. As the huge exposition ground on, I began to feel the painful beginning of that which was to come. Passages that had become exhilarating were agonizing. Like one of those awful dreams in which your feet seem glued to the ground, the infamous pages of octaves, skips, gargantuan arpeggios, and finale were simply torture.

And then, finally, thank God, it was over. I bowed quickly, walked to the dressing room and threw up. The stagehand called for me to take a second bow. I felt so foolish considering the performance I'd put in. Then, back to heaving. I then went straight to the Health Service where an X-ray revealed I had pneumonia.

Even without pneumonia, the "Mephisto Waltz" can betray veterans without warning. In fact, I've heard three big pianists struggle through performances of this big endurance problem. A friend of mine studied seven summers with Rachmaninoff near Paris. During each he heard the great Rachmaninoff practice the "Mephisto Waltz," although he never played it in public. When he finally asked Rachmaninoff why, he replied that he just couldn't get 'comfortable' with it. His wisdom as an artist meant that he knew better than to dare himself in front of an audience.

A fine performance is made by the quality of practice and preparation behind it. When this idea is fully understood, ideas such as 'good' or 'bad' days cease to be relevant. Sometimes, great performances can happen under less than good circumstances. When I studied at Oberlin, a big influence on my musical development was a lady by the name of Inda Howland, the Eurythmics teacher. Ms. Howland was an engaging, even intimidating, personality who often raised the ire of others on the faculty with the zeal of her convictions. But, to her credit, she had convictions and she lived them fully, not only musically, but personally.

Her favorite pianists were incredibly different, demonstrating that what was important to her were elements in the playing far below the surface. She worshipped Rachmaninoff and Gieseking. Once I asked her which was the greatest concert she had ever heard. To my astonishment she cited a recital on an Indian Reservation in the Southwest played by the great German pianist Edwin Fischer. In a small wooden building, maybe a meeting hall or a dining room perhaps, on an old, snaggle-toothed, upright piano, with every imaginable problem, the legendary romanticist played his heart out to a small but captivated group of equally unlikely listeners, none of whom would ever forget the experience.

Every artist encounters terrible instruments and situations from time to time. Sometimes one must change a program or alter the way in which it is presented, perhaps engaging the audience by speaking a bit. I learned during long tours, facing all possible conditions, that one's audience need not suffer for taking the time, interest, and money to attend your show. It's your job to create a musical experience regardless of the limitations.

Sometimes the purely unexpected can cause trouble for the performer, sometimes, with the best intentions. Frank Mannheimer left the United States as a young man to become a student of the great English pedagogue Tobias Matthey. In pre-war London he became part of a circle of fabulous young artists including Myra Hess and Clifford Curzon. In those days a promising young pianist in England was groomed for quite a long time, playing for various musical clubs, and of course, on the BBC, over the radio—frequently on very short notice. Since there were no cameras, music could and often was used with the aid of a reliable page-turner—perhaps the most thankless job in music.

Once while nervously awaiting the sign to begin, the young Frank Mannheimer sat perspiring at the piano in the BBC studios listening with his equally nervous page turner to the pre-performance remarks of a typically stoic BBC announcer. As the comments about Schubert and the big Wanderer Fantasy (which was about to be played) went on and on, Mr. Mannheimer started wondering if he'd be so nervous by the time a finger was finally pointed at him that he wouldn't be able to play at all.

In minute detail the announcer related the story of Schubert's own premiere performance of this huge and challenging work, describing his protracted efforts with the unwieldy first movement and as well with the climax of the second movement. In the third movement Schubert's pianistic limitations failed him completely when he got to the knotty fugue of the closing section. As Schubert collapsed on his third attempt, the announcer went on, " . . . and taking the score up from the piano and dashing it violently to the floor, Schubert leapt to his feet with fists clenched and screamed heavenward, 'May the devil himself play this piece! . . .' and now Frank Mannheimer will play the Wanderer Fantasy . . ."

As Mr. Mannheimer described it, the show did go on, but only after a significant interlude of recorded music during which everybody got control of their laughter.

Sometimes, even with all the hurdles of performance well managed, a well-wishing critic has the last surprising word. I've concluded that generally reviews should be gratefully used, quietly ignored, or, as in this case, cherished.

Shortly after World War II, Mr. Mannheimer performed on the big recital series in Kansas City where the local newspaper critic was both respected and feared. The day after the concert, Mr. Mannheimer was not above looking through the morning edition to see how his performance of the Brahms Handel Variations, greeted with a standing ovation by a full house, had fared with the critic. Toward the end of the review it read, "Frank Mannheimer's rendering of the Brahms Handel Variations was the apex of the musical season." Sadly, however, the typesetter at the newspaper mistakenly omitted the 'x' from apex.

Finally with all else imaginable accounted for, a pianist needs to be careful about the company he keeps at the piano. A clumsy or inexperienced page turner can cause all sorts of problems, usually dropping or fowling up the music, or in this case, due to a loose tongue.

Prior to another BBC Broadcast performance while Mr. Mannheimer waited with his page turner, a lady friend of some social standing, the intrepid announcer exhaustively conveyed every minutia of the storyline upon which Liszt's Mephisto Waltz is based. Finally he reached the end of the story as Mephistopheles grabs the girl, hauling her out of the inn and into the woods. With mock naiveté, as Mannheimer gave his hands a final wipe with his handkerchief, he leaned toward the page turner and softly said, "Why in heaven's name did they go off into the woods?" To which the lady politely responded, "To gather nuts, of course." Again the BBC had to rely on a bit of recorded music.

Sick or well, if you can crawl to the piano, you play. My teacher Aurora Underwood had a recital performance ending with Balakirev's "Islamey" on the very evening after badly slicing a right-hand finger with a butcher's knife. She used all her inventive powers to make a bandage for an injury that should have been stitched immediately and played the performance.

Following my radiation therapy, extreme dehydration caused several of my fingers to split open at the tips. Regardless of excruciating pain, my very best performance of the Tchaikovsky Concerto was concluded by a standing ovation and a blood-stained keyboard.

There are no small performances, only small audiences. During my Oberlin years, I would play a few recitals at colleges and universities when I returned home to Oregon for the Christmas holidays. Once, I arrived with my mother in Ashland at the extreme south end of the state and was greeted by the concert manager for Southern Oregon College, who began a long apology that my concert had been wrongly scheduled for the very same evening as the homecoming game and that he expected little or no audience. Over dinner he gave me my check and suggested that I not bother playing the recital and begin the long and probably foggy drive back to Portland early in the evening. Frankly, I would have loved to, but about two hours later I walked out on stage to be greeted by an audience of four people sitting together. In an effort to minimize the awkwardness, I thanked them for coming and chatted for a minute or two about the program … as if we were simply in a large living room together.

Omitting my break for intermission, for a program including Beethoven's Sonata Op. 2, No. 2, Ravel's "Gaspard de La Nuit" and the Brahms F minor Sonata Op. 5, I received the smallest standing ovation in music history.

Over the years my mother provided an absolutely reliable source of judgment about the general condition of my playing. Though fiercely loyal and absolutely supportive, no one in my life was more demanding. That recital in Ashland, Oregon remained in my mother's memory as among the very best performances she heard me play. Although we arrived back in Portland absolutely pooped in the wee hours of the morning, my persistence in performing for four people provided important lessons about what makes me tick and why I play the piano.

With Nothing to Lose, Try Starting from the Top

Having left New York, but still in my twenties, my efforts toward a career still came in spurts and stops. As I wondered about the necessity of returning to New York, I also did not miss the occasional ugly prejudices and poor ethics of the music business. At least now I was being judged more fairly and felt some justice that the quality of my playing determined my chances for success. As a result my playing continued to grow and I to happily mature.

During this period of playing to nearly anyone who would listen, after I played for the local conductor in Tucson, he said, "You know what you should do?" (Obvious answer: I had no idea whatsoever.) "You should go to Chicago and meet John Edwards, manager of the Chicago Symphony Orchestra. He's probably the most powerful man in American music, and you should just show him your stuff, ask him his advice. If he likes your playing, anything can happen."

It sounded ridiculous. But then, measured by the ridiculousness of my life, it seemed like the most normal and sensible thing in the world to do. Why not? But how?

This question would answer itself, as many do. Not long after, I was on a cross-country flight next to two guys that lived a couple of hours outside of Chicago. In the course of our conversation they asked me why I hadn't played with the Chicago Symphony. Before I knew it they were offering me the use of their apartment in Chicago in order for me to come and try to meet Edwards. As soon as I could I called them to accept the invitation. A key was left with the doorman as I flew to Chicago without a plan. I thank these people and the many others who have fed me and given me a place to stay—a regular orphan in the storm of my own brewing.

The next morning I gathered my courage and called the symphony office. Suddenly I found myself talking to John Edwards. Just as suddenly he asked if I could see him in an hour. Edwards and his equally large wooden office desk looked like one piece of furniture. I told him that I simply did not know what to do. Here I was with a big repertoire, lots of good reviews, several big contests in my credits, and very little happening. I felt as if no one cared how well I played.

John Edwards, 'the most powerful man in the business,' also one of the busiest, spent over an hour with me that day. He looked at my reviews from Europe and raised his eyebrows. "I think Solti would find these reviews interesting," he mumbled. Then he looked up, "We're coming to New York in a few weeks—why don't you play for me there. If I like it, I'll ask Solti to hear you."

I'd wondered if those recitals in Europe would ever amount to a hill of beans. But then, John Edward's furry eyebrows were up. When I returned to New York, I went to see the house manager of Carnegie Hall and explained my opportunity. I was generously given an hour for an audition while Edwards and the Chicago Symphony were in town, during which I could audition.

I prepared Bach's Chromatic Fantasy and Fugue, the lovely Brahms Variations in D Major on an Original Theme, and the Mephisto Waltz. When I finished he told me he'd talk to Solti and arrange for an audition. This much of the story represents the easy part. Nailing down a man like Solti for an audition is probably harder than meeting the president of the United States. Over the next several months, I made no less than five trips to Chicago to play for him. Each time the schedule just collapsed, or he was so rushed and harried that Edwards thought it not advisable. I liked and trusted him, and simply did as he said.

Suddenly in the early spring there were lots of phone calls to my manager. A date was set, then canceled. Then another—and again canceled. And then silence. And more silence. There seemed no reason not to go on a two week Caribbean Cruise engagement I'd just been offered. I called Edwards to make sure I could play at sea.

On the very day I returned to New York, I received word from Edwards that in forty-eight hours I would play for Solti in Chicago. After an early morning flight to Chicago, I arrived at Symphony Hall and met a young woman in a fur coat. It became obvious she would also play when she asked to go first. She'd auditioned for a special Chicago Symphony committee and was the only one in some time to be recommended to Solti. I wanted to chat, but she wouldn't have a thing to do with me. She was mature and very confident. I felt sure that we would be compared.

I didn't really listen to her play, but did want to know what she'd do. All her pieces were big and noisy. Twenty minutes later she came downstairs and told me it was my turn. I wondered what to play first, pondering that everyone must open with technically impressive repertoire. I figured if you've gotten this far, you have to have 'chops.' Besides, Solti was a fine pianist. Not wanting to be a technical showoff in the eyes of another pianist, I hoped to win his attention and perhaps sympathies as a musician. I'd open with the Beethoven Op. 101.

This particular Sonata has a little first movement that is deceptively sweet and simple in character. But one could go a lifetime and never hear it played with just the right child-like nostalgia yet without a trace of sentimentality. Considering legato, phrasing, balance, rhythmic nuance, rubato, line, and subtlety of style, it is the toughest musical three pages of the Beethoven Sonatas.

I climbed a small circular staircase and fumbled my way forward to what I thought was the door to the stage. When I opened it, I saw a tangle of chairs and music stands from rehearsal and beyond, a piano. Then I saw Solti standing in front of the platform. He wore a camel-colored roll neck sweater and looked very grave. But when I got closer, he looked so much like my beloved teacher, Frank Mannheimer, that my fears began to fade. I bent down and shook his hand over the edge of the platform.

"Vaht vill you play?"

"Opus 101" is all I said. To another pianist the 'Beethoven' and the 'Sonata' part was assumed.

An enormous smile came across his face as he said, "Ah, good," and scrambled back to take a seat mid-hall. I adjusted my bench and took a deep breath. Just as I was ready to play he screamed, "Take your time. Get used to piano if you vant to."

I was caught just about to start, and I smiled a little awkwardly and said, "I'm OK. Thanks."

I played the first movement—only about two minutes. Just as I finished the last sweet cadence, I heard his voice just to my right.

"Beautiful. Very good." He looked at me with both surprise and warmth now, no longer talking to me as a stranger. I felt myself blush.

"Theese is very deevicult. I think the hardest movement of all, musically. You are very gifted."

Gladdened by my choice, I looked down in order to conceal an enormous smile which threatened to remain in place indefinitely.

"Vood you like to play some more?"

"Well, I prepared the whole Sonata, some Bach, some —" he cut me off.

"I vood like to have you play vith the Chicago Symphony. Vat Concerti do you know?" I named my favorites.

"Now, could you play the second movement? I'd like to hear vaht you do. Don't worry, I like you. I'm just interested."

Then he laughed as if caught in a little lie. "I vant to see if you have beeg sound, too."

About four measures did the trick. I have a big sound, sometimes too big.

Needless to say, I was elated by all this. It would take a few months during which the next season was scheduled until I could be fit in as a soloist for three subscription concerts. This was of no concern, because of the importance that I would be the first young artist chosen by audition ever to be presented on subscription concerts with the Chicago Symphony.

When a possibility came along, a call came in suggesting I do the Shostakovich 2nd. It had never been done there, and there was a good program in which to include it. I didn't know it at all. I'd answer in twenty-four hours. I ran to the library and brought it home to read through. Almost instantly I knew that it was all wrong for me. I called back and apologized, but I just couldn't settle for a work I didn't like.

As I contemplated the fact that over one-hundred years of guest pianists had been coming and going in Chicago without a single performance of the Shostakovich 2nd, it seemed that there was likely a good reason for its neglect. I quietly clung to my courage and waited.

Forty eight hours later, a call came.

"Mark," I was told, "Sir Georg has put you on a program. You will play the Ravel G Major. This isn't up for discussion."

Discussion?—not only a great piece but right up my alley. On this appearance so much would ride. Enthusiasts would have confirmation and skeptics, perhaps a nudge towards acceptance.

As a result of my time on the Caribbean ship I was offered the chance to play aboard the Queen Elizabeth II. The Q.E.II was huge, classy, with a wonderful food service to match. There, I had a seven-foot Steinway in a small theater and kept company with a baritone from the Metropolitan Opera and his wife. Our recitals shared the theater with showings of films accompanied by two of their big stars, Van Johnson, and the still beautiful Moira Shearer of the classic film, The Red Shoes.

With my beautiful but somewhat shy sister, Martha, I enjoyed two weeks dining with Van and his manager, Ms. Shearer and her husband, the captain with a different guest each meal, and the Met baritone and his diamond clad wife. One evening during dinner, wearing a stunning new white silk brocade dress just made for her in Hong Kong, Shearer was telling a story. At the punch line, her hand gesture brought a glass of red wine right into her lap. As the others at the table gasped and lurched forward, she tossed her napkin gamely into her lap and finished the joke without dropping a syllable. And after a huge laugh, she deftly excused herself to return only minutes later in an identical dress of another color. Cool.

For the companion to a performer, being tethered to the center of so much attention can be both fun and problematic. During the cruise I was often made quite a fuss over by the members of my audience as we met on deck. Martha and I played blackjack every night after dinner. I can make twenty dollars last a long time but am rarely better than that. One would sit, the other standing behind, kibitzing mid cruise, when a beautiful woman from Brazil, accompanied onboard by her equally ravishing daughters, came over to our table. After excusing herself, she asked me if she could 'steal' my 'wife' away for part of the evening, as she and her daughters had been admiring her beauty and charm for days and wanted the chance to speak with her. I've always relished that lovely compliment to my sister.

Our one day on land was in Los Angeles. (Martha and I boarded in Honolulu and would fly home from Acapulco.) So what do you do with a rental car and one long day in L.A.? Well, prior to Magic Mountain and a dozen roller coasters, we stopped by Beverly Hills to join a friend for lunch at a funny little place with an exercise room behind. I'd heard a little about the maniac who ran it, but nothing could prepare us for our first glimpse of the improbable Richard Simmons. Coming by our table for a quick "hello," we talked for only a couple of minutes when suddenly he jumped up right onto our table and ran, table by table, across the room and across everyone's lunch, diving straight into the arms of Clint Eastwood who'd just appeared at the far door. That was my first introduction to the improbable Mr. Simmons. As zany as he seemed, I soon discovered the ironclad intelligence behind the façade.

With the Ravel Concerto learned earlier in the season and performed several times with smaller orchestras on my way to Chicago, when I finally found myself walking onto the platform of Symphony Hall for my first of three subscription concerts I was smiling so broadly it hurt. I was sandwiched in between one of the world's best orchestras and one of the world's most spoiled publics. The fallboard on the German Steinway was like a black mirror. As I looked at it and saw my onyx shirt studs, I reached for a handkerchief in my breast pocket and glanced up to the warm, wise eyes of first cellist Frank Miller. On his face was a fatherly smile. I wiped my hands and put them on my knees, looking up at Sir

Georg, who was fiddling with his shirt cuffs, and nodded 'ready.'

The manager Jacques Leiser used to say that there is no 'first' or 'last' performance, just 'the latest' performance on which one builds. But as I sat on that platform, heart pounding, the low rumble of an expectant audience on the right, I knew that his words were not true. I needed, both for my reputation and for Mr. Solti's faith in me, a big, unqualified success. To my delight I received three standing ovations over the next three nights and a terrific review.

The afternoon after the third performance, I was walking near the Water Tower after lunch. The sky was bright blue and the air cold. Suddenly I heard the squeal of brakes and lurched around to see a car stop in the middle of the street and a man stick his head out of the window and yell, "Hey, Westcott, you were great last night." I felt like a big-league baseball player. Chicago's got heart.

A moment later I found myself in a little book store. Coming around a stack of fiction, I ran into Richard Simmons. I began to stammer, "Hi," and explain that we had met briefly years back at his restaurant, when he cut me off saying, "Oh yes. Mark the pianist, isn't it?" There's a lesson in that.

I had a date with myself to practice underneath the stage of Orchestra Hall for the second performance, and as I headed south along Michigan Avenue I passed hundreds of people, each with different destinations and cares. I felt both happy and sad. Everything seemed different— neither better nor worse, just different. I was a little farther along and despite the difficulties of the business, the frequent pain of rejection and neglect, or the blinding joys of occasional successes. Despite all of it, perhaps even despite myself, I was growing up.

On the Road Again

As a result of my performances with Solti, I soon became very busy and began to learn first-hand the joys and tribulations of a busy concert schedule. Whether or not I was professionally and personally ready would be thoroughly tested.

I suppose that being a bit of a 'ham' could be among the necessary ingredients of being a successful concert performer. There's no doubt that sometimes in front of the public one feels as if he is all but making something, perhaps even a very great deal, out of little or nothing.

Playing music is like storytelling; there is a logical sequence of events that takes the listener from the beginning to the end. Just as a fine actor never loses character, a concert performer must have a firm grip on an underlying core from which the piece evolves—not the notes, but that which we sense they are describing. This unfolding story holds our attention by the strength of style and drama—an atmosphere that pervades both large and small. Pungent, even mesmerizing in the hands of a fine artist, it can be conveyed by means so subtle as to seem all but undetectable. Even the most restrained or dignified of concert personalities have understood that even the classical artist is just as much a pure performer or entertainer as a rocker, or even the gentleman working a crowd in a side show.

In the worst turbulence of my flying experience, I drew on those very instincts in an effort to keep a difficult experience from becoming an absolute nightmare during a wintertime flight from Richmond, Virginia to Boston. When I boarded the plane, I was sandwiched between two huge gentlemen who were apparently among the members of a professional ice hockey team, I believe from Chicago. The team members made up the majority of the passengers on this little jet into which we were all crammed like sardines. I soon realized that party time was at hand, and must have been so for the previous leg of this flight to the tune of at least two, if not three cocktails for most of the players. After takeoff the crew blithely served up yet another round before the in flight dinner. I included myself among the orders in an attempt to survive the cramped and noisy merriment.

About the time everyone had taken only a few sips, the plane entered a violent storm which would last for the duration of the two-hour flight. A seatbelt was barely adequate as the plane pitched and rocked, sometimes slamming down as if against pavement, at other times wafting with nearly endless periods of weightlessness. What helped me along was a little bit of personal knowledge that I now coveted after having survived so many salmon fishing excursions with my father on the violent and dangerous bar of the Columbia River. That crossing is perhaps the most dangerous bar in North America, claiming literally thousands of shipwrecks including state-of-the-art Coast Guard vessels capsized and sunk in the act of attempting to rescue others!

All of us eager salmon fishermen earned our sea legs in the late August of several summers by exploring the many and various shades of green to which one can actually turn, diverting from the lighthearted activities of ramming large hooks into one's hand while handling ice-cold and slippery herring, or simply trying to stay sitting upright, much less standing, in a vessel that would make any looping roller coaster seem like a rocking chair.

Sometimes we would lose lunch in choruses, like a strange group of aliens singing in some queer guttural language, emanating not from our vocal chords but from recesses hitherto unknown. Sometimes in canon, duets, trios—every conceivable combination, there was always someone who wanted to be a soloist, and for them, a special part of verse returning to the colloquial English was reserved: "Fish on," as they would wrench their pole upward to set the hook in the salmon's jaw and lunge headfirst over the side of the boat, punctuating their excitement with one more explosion.

As my mind returned to my growing predicament between two behemoth hockey players, a faint smile drifted over my face as I felt actually a bit lucky to be in that plane, not in a twenty two foot fishing boat tossing violently on the waters of the Columbia bar. And then it wandered back again . . .

One great mystery lingered unsolved for several annual pilgrimages to minute Chinook, Washington, in pursuit of the mighty salmon. How did my father, year after year, manage not only to avoid sea sickness but to actually enjoy himself during those torturous, all day outings—going so far as to feast repeatedly on salami sandwiches washed down with beer? His only apparent risk seemed that of choking while he was eating and laughing uproariously at the convulsions of otherwise sedate people who had naively said yes to an invitation for a day of fishing. How did he do it?

Finally one summer—as a matter of fact, the last during which I would subject myself to this ordeal—the answer came. We had just arrived at Chinook, a little over two-hour drive from Portland. At seven p.m., with just a little bit of daylight remaining, my father excused himself, saying that before we unloaded and set up a tent he'd like to go down and just take a look at the moorage. Paying no particular attention, after a few seconds I decided to join him and walked briskly about a hundred feet behind.

When Dad abruptly stopped on the road I could see him straighten up and lift his head skyward with the suddenness of a cognition not unlike that of a wild animal smelling danger in the wind. After only a couple seconds of filling his lungs to capacity with sea air, he turned toward the edge of the road and without so much as a millisecond's hesitation threw up in the bushes.

The whole thing was done with a ceremonial succinctness that left no doubt in my young mind that at this very moment, like in all the preceding summers, my father was making peace with the sea gods, relieving himself of the kind of fears, anxieties, or other encumbrances that make normal people more susceptible to seasickness.

When I caught up to him, I was laughing so hard that I could barely speak and pointed an accusative finger, shouting, "So that's how you do it! Just wait till I tell everybody how you do it. Year after year you go out and watch people turn themselves inside and out with every shade of green imaginable and you laugh your head off. Now I know how you do it. Just wait till I tell everybody what you do. It's great, but criminal in a way."

My father was easy to both hate and love; so on learning his secret, everyone ridiculed him mercilessly, and he enjoyed the episode enormously. I admired the simple wisdom of his approach and remembered the results.

Again I awakened from my recollections, this time to an eerie silence in a plane that just moments before had resounded in deafening revelry. Just then, a number of heads in the very first row disappeared and the terrible sound of big men puking on their shoes carried down the aisle of the airplane. No one said a word. But you could feel an enormous collective cringing among all of the other teammates and passengers.

Just then the heads in the second row disappeared. Again, the sound of a slaughterhouse tape recorded and played backwards—an indescribably awful sound prompting a deepening collective cringe. Row by row in relentless rhythm this plague marched along, wafting like an invisible wave over the heads of its helpless victims. The third row—goners. A little more silence and wham, the plane hit a huge air pocket—fourth row, down for the count. If I didn't take action with the men on both sides overflowing into my tiny domain, my fate was certain. Perhaps if I could gain their trust and redirect their attention, I could save them and thus myself.

Quietly, with an air of the importance with which one reveals a valuable secret I whispered, "Would you guys like to know a sure fire way not to get sick?" Without a moment's hesitation I had their attention as I employed every bit of performer's hokum at my disposal.

"Well, put your hands on the back of the seat in front of you and pretend that it's the shoulders of the captain and co pilot. Now close your eyes. Now, imagine that you're standing right behind the pilot or co pilot and while gently resting your hands on the shoulders, look out, out, out into the distance ahead of the plane. Just barely you see the lights of Logan Field in Boston as they beckon the plane toward the runway."

The three of us sat as if meditating while the rest of the passengers went pathological—puking and groaning. Like three religious ascetics we sat with our eyes closed, resting our hands on the seatbacks in front of us.

Quietly I repeated, "See the lights. See them pulling the plane forward. That's where we're going to land. Just keep looking out straight in front. Look out into the distance. Feel the calmness, we're all right. Let the plane bounce around, we're still going forward, we're still heading toward our target."

For the next two or three minutes, with as much soothing calm as I could muster, reassurances of our eminent arrival by a beckoning destination became my mantra. To my delight, my rambling was soon interrupted as one of my neighbors chirped, "I think I feel better." And indeed, the other joined in to what started as a duet and became a trio of ever-raising spirits and growing relief.

My little make believe mental picture, mimicking a tried but true visual aid of focusing on a faraway and stable object, had helped. Before long, we were enjoying ourselves with increasing gusto and finished our drinks as the wave of nausea we had once been dreading passed over our row, crashing down on the innocent, less enlightened victims behind.

From then until our descent into the Boston area, we could barely contain our snickering as we wheezed with laughter over the spasms of row after row behind. To keep our spirits high, our confidence strong, and our thoughts merry under the circumstances, we weren't about to question the airplane etiquette of having a little laugh in the face of the misery that we avoided. Upon arriving in Boston, my two colleagues escorted me off the plane with the warmth and ceremony of a departing dignitary. I was a little embarrassed by their effusive gratitude, particularly since they seemed to extend mercilessly the ritual in the presence of their teammates still reeling in expletive-laden laments about the nature of our flight and their condition.

When I made my way to the escalators and baggage claim, I must have been smiling broadly as I descended while many crossing my path in the opposite direction smiled back. I grabbed my bag, dashed outside, and clambered into the back seat of a taxi.

"One-ninety nine, Commonwealth Avenue, the Saint Botolph Club, please."

"Which way would you like me to go?" the cabdriver snorted over his shoulder in a heavy Boston accent.

"The tunnel, of course," I said almost unconsciously.

As I pondered the days ahead and my arrival at the Club, where I would have the privilege of staying in a small suite of lovely old fashioned rooms and eating like a king by the blessing of Mario's superb cooking, all thoughts of the ordeal from which I had just narrowly extricated myself had faded from my mind.

Then it hit me: a veritable wall of the foulest, most acidic and thoroughly asphyxiating odor. I looked up with eyes already beginning to redden and a throat closing with irritation to see us pulling to a stop in the mid tunnel behind seemingly endless rows of cars, all fully stopped and belching hurricanes of noxious emissions as they rattled and vibrated in the darkness of the tunnel.

I was in commuter hell. Any smile had vanished from my face, and as I asked the driver if he knew what was up, he nonchalantly leaned his head over against a hand perched on crooked elbow, leaning against his door—all as if to say, "Forget griping; this happens all the time."

And at that instant I would have taken a deep sigh under any less noxious circumstances and leaned back in my seat, perhaps even for a few minutes' nap. Instead, my mouth had suddenly become a torrent of saliva that seemed to come from everywhere all at the same time. And just about when I thought I'd choke, that certain and terrible knowledge blazed into my mind as if in neon, and I rolled down the cab window with a circular blur of both hands clenching the defenseless knob, stuck my head out of the window, and let her rip.

Logan Tunnel, one—Mark, nothing.

Much concert related travel would be just as gruesome and difficult. Sometimes less than an hour following a tough flight or horrific ferry crossing, for example in New Zealand's turbulent Cook Straight, I'd find myself walking out before an audience with a smile on my face.

Mexico

The old phrase "be careful what you wish for" applied constantly to the mishaps and difficulties I encountered on tour. Mastering and maintaining my pieces often took second place to surviving a labyrinth of cultural, legal, personal, and even biological challenges. My first visit to Mexico was no exception.

South of the Rio Grande, the music business can become pretty weird. Stories abound about artists never paid for whole tours in Mexico, Central, and South America. And the pianos! Experienced artists often tell you to get a large part of your fee up front . . . or just don't go. My first tour of recitals in Mexico was a little monster. I had to play twelve recitals in six days—twice a day, at noon and at eight p.m., each at different university campuses around Mexico City. Driving to some seemed all but endless in a nightmare of stifling heat, world-famous air pollution, and the most awful traffic congestion imaginable. At each locale I encountered mobs of clambering, jabbering, and even hostile kids.

A couple of days into the week's concerts, I found myself short of funds. Although I was contracted to be paid only $500 (U.S.) for each, with two shows per day for only a week's work, I would receive $6,000.

I called to ask for half my fee. A messenger arrived only an hour later saying he was prepared to pay me the whole fee, but as he counted out the cash, I noticed I was being paid five-hundred pesos for each of twelve concerts—not dollars. Chicken feed. With growing concern, I politely produced my contract, pointing out the specification of U.S. dollars. The messenger went ashen. Waiting through a long phone call in Spanish, I understood that I had a big problem on my hands. Ready to pack and leave, I called the U.S. Embassy. The next morning an efficient looking woman delivered $6,000 with a request that I say nothing and just play my concerts. Uncle Sam comes through.

The Hotel Geneva, located in what's called the Zona Rosa, became my sanctuary. Surrounded by blocks of little international shops and restaurants, my return each evening felt like a rescue from Hell itself.

Each evening I reported the day's horrors to a buddy from Portland who was tagging along. Free from my miseries and happily enjoying carefree days as a tourist, his only problem was that no matter how diligently we kept all the windows closed, one overzealous mosquito would find its way into the room. I just hate that moment, as you're falling asleep, when suddenly what sounds like a Boeing 747 flies into your ear. Every night there was one—just one. Soon, what continued as Ken's torment evolved to my delight.

Accustomed to sleeping without a shirt, and in Mexico City's heat finding blankets too hot, Ken must have seemed like a banquet to our resident predator. As I read by the nightstand light, I'd glance from time to time over to his slumbering chest waiting to catch sight of our guest. Just as the little bugger would land on him, wham, down came my reading material on my poor startled friend. My only effort to excuse such poor behavior was to produce a tiny corpse while laughing uncontrollably. Not nice. With Pavlovian certainty, over only the next few nights while I read and waited, Ken's slumber would suddenly be interrupted as he lurched up with a yell. What had I done?

Visible from my hotel, high above gigantic Reforma Boulevard, stood a magnificent golden angel atop a tall marble column. Alone and remote from the daily mix of tourists and beggars she glistened golden in warm sunlight, and by night was bathed in the cool pale blue of a beguiling Latin moon. Silent and perfect, tempted only to answer from her conception to God himself (perhaps her only neighbor) though regal and aloof, on one night, through her serene gaze I sensed a deep sadness. At that moment, perhaps secretly hoping herself to walk on the warm pavement below, while no less the goddess of her domain, she was the prisoner of her virtue.

Circling her head each night was a tiny bat, her faithful but only companion. Not forged of the same fiery purity of his queen, the little bat shared the same lofty perspective of the world and the people below. In fact it was her glistening magnificence creating the lure to a feast of nightly insects for her small friend which invited his company. Whatever the reason, the grace of their nightly union was the simple pleasure of a companion.

Running through this ordeal was the added challenge of a couple of medical problems. Because of the dirty piano keys, I awakened very alarmed in the middle of one night with bright red streaks running up both arms. I'd scraped the third fingers of my hands while playing a double glissando in Liszt's Mephisto Waltz. (Ever since then, I routinely wash the piano keys before any concert I play.) At about three a.m., I was visited by a U.S. military doctor who gave me a shot in the butt and put me on antibiotics.

A word to the wise: when in a foreign country, if in need of a doctor call an American military base or find a Swiss doctor—especially in England.

Now playing with two fingers that felt like bamboo shoots were being driven under the nails, I was encountering tricky problems in dealing with the 'trots.' As the days ground on, and life itself seemed to drain from me, my tempos became faster and my breaks from the piano more frequent. As my final concert at the University for American Studies was going to be attended by the president of Mexico and his wife, who was a big piano fan, I wanted to play well. When I asked about some medication for my dilemma, I was provided with some little white Lomotil pills. Unfortunately, they made me very high, and I played the weirdest Chromatic Fantasy and Fugue of Bach ever, and a disgustingly sentimental Chopin Barcarolle. The Piano Sonata by Donald Keats was nearly unintelligible, but after a welcome meditation in the loo during most of the intermission, I played the best darned Beethoven "Appassionata" Sonata of my life. No telling.

The next day Ken and I rushed to Puerto Vallarta to recover. Checking into the hotel, we discovered that the taxi driver had snitched my canvas tote bag. As with so much in the preceding days, even for a small-time thief this too would be a fiasco, for in that little bag had been stowed all my terrifying underwear from the week of diarrhea before.

As the hotel manager hurriedly began to call the police, I grabbed his hand, trying to explain the greeting that awaited the taxi driver. Due to all the newspaper pictures with the president and his wife from the preceding night's concert, our arrival at the hotel had been greeted by a formal lineup of all the employees suitable for arriving dignitaries. As the manager passed on the details of the robbery and its loot, the staff began—like dominos, one by one—to double over in hysterics.

After this auspicious arrival, Ken and I were most interested in grabbing a couple of hours on the beach. At dusk we wearily returned to our room to find an enormous bouquet of flowers and a splendid collection of food and wine, sent compliments of the management. But, best of all was a large box on my bed containing two-dozen pairs of brand new Jockey shorts—just my size.

Sometimes funny but more often sad, poverty and pilfering seem ever present in Mexico's large population of the poor. While traveling in Mexico, the elderly mother of a couple from Portland had succumbed to the heat and died very suddenly in a small village. They rolled the body in a large rug and tied the bundle atop their station wagon and began the long drive toward the airport. After a hot morning's drive they stopped for a cold drink at the town square of a little town. Just moments away from their car, they returned to discover the rug and its contents gone. If my taxi driver got a surprise, imagine the one which greeted those rug thieves.

Down, But Not Under

When I was invited to play a major tour sponsored by Australia's government-funded concert commission, I couldn't imagine the supreme test I would face. With over two dozen concerts in only six weeks, I prepared carefully for what would be a real juggling act. There would be four concertos: Brahms 1st, Rachmaninoff Paganini Variations, Saint Saëns No.2, and the Barber Piano Concerto. There were also about a dozen performances of a recital program including the Chromatic Fantasy and Fugue of Bach, Poulenc's Movement Perpetuels, Beethoven's Sonata Op. 110, the Scriabin 9th Sonata, and three pieces of Liszt from Années de Pèlerinage: Sonetto No. 104, Au Bord d'une Source, and Vallee d'Obermann—plus encores including the dazzling and difficult Caprice Espagnol by Moszkowski.

I arranged a ten-day, pre-tour working vacation in Honolulu. Staying at the apartment of a friend from the faculty of the University of Hawaii, I'd swim, practice and rest before what promised to be a grueling six weeks. Despite my efforts to guarantee being at my best, the fates had other plans. Not one hour out of San Francisco, I began to feel those awful aches and pains, accompanied by the chills and fever that signal a substantial attack of the flu. By the time we landed in Honolulu I was really sick. Never before had I been unable to fulfill concert engagements due to illness, but this flu affected my inner ear and sense of balance so drastically that I was barely able to negotiate myself to the bathroom, much less make my way to the practice studio awaiting me at the university.

Day after awful day I lay forty stories up, frantically anticipating nine consecutive concerts with three different concertos scheduled in the Sydney Opera House which began my tour. As the days ground on, I didn't seem any better. In near desperation I called the ABC (Australian Broadcasting Commission) to give them the bad news. However, Australia is not the kind of place to which substitutes just hop down on a commuter flight to fill in for a sick artist. It became apparent that if I had to be raised from the dead and wheeled to the piano, I would play.

What saved my neck was a hand exercise my father taught me. Dad was a successful and well-known collegiate wrestling coach, producing an N.C.A.A. Championship team as well as participants in the World and Olympic Games. His expertise was the source of many training tricks that served me well as I was growing up. Every day, to keep my hands supple and strong, I wadded up mounds of newspapers, grabbing a full sheet by a corner, slowly pulling it in until it was all within the grasp of my hand. I did this as many times as I could. Once a day, score in hand, I played mentally through one concerto and a quarter of my recital program. With blazing fevers I persisted in this ritual for over a week.

By God's grace, the very day of my flight to Sydney I was just well enough to take a cab up to the university and struggle through all of forty minutes of light practice. That evening at midnight I left for Sydney. I was comfortably bedded down in four seats in the front row of the darkened business class sleeping the whole way.

Arriving in Sydney, following a short nap, I summoned the strength to go to the ABC studios for what was the most arduous day of practice of my entire life. When I could do no more I hoped that I might feel a little better when I greeted the orchestra at rehearsal the next morning.

On a day that should have been one of the finest of my young career, I arrived at the beautiful Sydney Opera House shivering with chills and aching from head to toe. Of course the conductor, a superb musician and gentleman named Louis Fremeux, knew about my malady, suggesting that I should mock through rehearsal in order to save energy before the evening's performance. Nevertheless I arrived home unable to eat lunch and feeling worse than ever. I laid my concert clothes out, feeling that I would awaken from my afternoon nap better prepared to go to my execution than my Sydney Debut with the Brahms 1st Concerto.

That evening I was ceremoniously shown to what would be my dressing room for the next two weeks. As the door shut behind me, I put my bags down, turned off all but one light, sat in a chair, put my elbows down on the make up desk, looking into the mirror momentarily, then bowed my head, folded my hands and prayed for all I was worth. Busy atoning for everything I'd ever done, I spotted an envelope with my name on it. From a Portland couple on an Australian vacation, I had in fact grown up with both of their children and had even been to their home. Expressing their incredible surprise at having arrived in Sydney to see my name all over town, they would be in row X fondly cheering on one of their own.

When Mr. Fremeux came to my warm up room and led me to the edge of the stage, where I would walk out to begin the first half of the opening concert for the Sydney Symphony, I must have looked awful, for at that moment he registered real concern on his face. With his hand on my shoulder, we walked very slowly as I listened obediently to his instructions. I was not to push. He had already instructed the orchestra to cut all the dynamic levels in half. Because we would play a little quietly, saving for only a few big moments, we might want to let the tempo move a little bit more than normal, relying on sweep, rather than the Brahmsian broadness that requires more sonority and strength than I had up my shirt sleeves.

When we got to the edge of the stage, he turned and said, "I know I sound concerned, but from the rehearsal I know you can do this. I must admit I was really surprised, because I know how ill you've been. But it's all there as long as fear doesn't take over." He continued, "I will do this performance. Be a good boy; don't be a star—not tonight, you're too sick." Just before we went out, he said, "Besides," and he began to smile very broadly, "it'll all be over in fifty-five minutes anyway, so what the hell?" and we walked out.

Every head in the orchestra was turned my direction, every face smiling, and as soon as I heard the magnificent opening phrase, I began to relax and feel better. I knew what I was doing so I folded my hands, put my head down, listened, and waited for my entrance. By the end of the piece, I had forgotten about being ill, and though I felt totally drained, my fever had vanished.

The Sydney newspapers are famous for taking American pianists, in particular, to the woodshed. To my astonishment, the reviews and the receptions of the following nights were all very good. I would leave Sydney feeling that horrible ordeal through which I had passed, long behind me.

I'd had such a rough time in Sydney that the stage manager of the concert hall called a friend in Brisbane asking if I might be put up in his home just for a couple of days. Especially on a long tour, staying in a private home, under the right circumstances, can really be a blessing. My host was a doctor and had managed a bit of time off for the days I stayed with him, even taking me to the nearby beach for a small but much needed break from the relentless pressure.

But after a couple of days I moved to a hotel perched on a hill just above the Brisbane Concert Hall, separated only by a large and heavily forested city park. Now I was well rested and excited about the upcoming Australian premiere of the Barber Piano Concerto. Like most Australian orchestras, the Brisbane Orchestra was somewhat ill-at-ease with the rhythmic demands of some twentieth century music; but the conductor, who, in the name of fairness, I will not name, was way out of his area of experience. Having made his mark primarily in the opera houses of England and Europe conducting the operas of Verdi and Puccini, his instincts were all of the right order, but his baton technique and attention to rhythmic detail were non existent.

What transpired was an orchestra reading a complicated score by which they were totally befuddled, led by a flamboyant conductor, huffing and puffing and waving his arms every which way in the air, while screaming obscene retributions ever more loudly at the orchestra. At one point he took off his glasses, shook his head in disgust, and said to me under his breath but audible to all, "I just don't know how they'll do it. They just have no idea."

With that, I asked for a moment to speak with him. I suggested that regardless of the next evening's performance, it might be good to rehearse a bit dry and under tempo, just to play in time and together. He agreed, returning to the podium to announce his version of my suggestion. However, as we picked it up, nothing had changed. Now clear that he simply hadn't studied the score thoroughly, soon the negative remarks began again, blaming the orchestra by sections, and then individuals, for a situation that simply was not their fault. By then, I'm sure the veins in my neck could have been visible a city block away. I was considering asking for another powwow when he threw his baton down, raging at the orchestra, "It's hopeless. You'll never get it!"

At that point I turned to the concert master saying, "I would like to be excused." Nodding, the concert master stood up, I stood up, and with that, the rest of the orchestra put down their instruments, stood, and began to walk out of the rehearsal room, leaving the conductor alone and dumbstruck with his tantrum. The conductor went limp with an expression of betrayal. As I stood at the piano, he finally turned to me and said, "What is going on?" Gathering my anger, I said, "Maestro, One is down, two is over to the left side, three is over to the right side, and four is up. You do it with your stick cleanly and in time so that people know where the damned beats are. All this flamboyant fan dancing might be fine with a score that doesn't call for much more than boom chick, but with something like this, you'd better know the score and convey it concisely and clearly to your people, or we're all going to have a disaster on our hands."

"Are you telling me that I am not conducting this work competently?"

Now I was laughing, "The only thing missing from your conducting are high heels, a sequined dress, big hair, and a feather boa!"

I guess that did it. He snatched up his scores and walked off in a huff toward his room. When I knocked politely on the door after many seconds I heard a quiet but stern, "Come in." I shut the door behind me and said, "I want to apologize for my characterization. I was completely out of line."

He turned to me saying, with a mix of chagrin and half smiling, "Not altogether. What the hell am I going to do?"

Diplomatically I said, "Let's take a look at the score together and see if we can turn this around."

For a half hour, I employed every bit of tact at my disposal (a quality for which I am not renowned) and must say, with considerable respect, that his attitude, deportment, and improvement from then until our performance the following evening, was no less than miraculous.

One special problem remained for which neither of us had a ready solution. The trombone section was simply unable to play the theme of the last movement in 5/8. It requires a quarter and three eighths every measure, but their inexperience with playing in odd meters made it impossible for them not to make it a dotted quarter and three eighths—playing it in exact 6/8 time. This made things a bit of a hat trick, to say the least, since not only the piano but other parts of the orchestra played the tune in canon against their unique presentation of Barber's intended rhythm.

Over and over, the conductor tried to convey their wrongdoing. But this particular group of union men was just not about to get it. As a last ditch effort, I asked to be excused for a brief moment to call the composer. To be perfectly honest, I didn't call the composer at all but went out to the hallway and went through all the motions of making a very long, complicated, and nosy call halfway around the world to New York City, going into a very cordial conversation with my friend Sam Barber.

On my return, the orchestra was beaming as if hearing a message from royalty; I told the trombone players that Mr. Barber had authorized that they were to play two eighth notes instead of the first quarter, with an accent on the first. After all, it's one thing to be thrown off by a long note and a bunch of short notes, but it's another not to be able to count up to five. They got it, and I was happy to leave it that way for the performance.

One thing not mentioned in most Australian tourism pamphlets is the enormous fruit bat population inhabiting every tree from Sydney northward. Fruit bats are the size of a large house cat, with a wing span of several feet, smell horrific (even from the ground), and shriek noisily throughout most of the day and night. Despite their menacing appearance, they are considered by the locals with nonchalance, insisting that the dear beasties are never aggressive and thoroughly harmless. They simply shriek too loud, crap all over, and smell terrible.

Unknowingly I was enjoying walks through the parks of Sydney and Brisbane in relative peace of mind. That is, until the night of the Samuel Barber Piano Concerto Premiere. About half past seven, upon leaving my hotel and walking toward the car and driver waiting for me, I passed by a group of very loaded Texan businessmen singing (very badly) the

Star Spangled Banner at the top of their lungs with drinks in hand. Smiling, I stopped to ask what all the patriotism was about. I was enthusiastically informed that in just moments the very first orbit of the very first space shuttle would pass over Brisbane, and we would be able to see it.

Suddenly there it was. And for ninety seconds we all respectfully *oooh*ed and awed as it darted distantly across the sky above. When all of our thoughts drifted back to *terra firma*, the four Texans inquired about my formal clothes. When I pointed out that it was another first, they all had to come hear it. I instructed my driver to take them, with my note, to the box office and to see that they were greeted by the hall manager who would then give them seats and instructions on how to come back to my dressing room at intermission. Handing the driver my jacket and briefcase, I decided to walk through the park down to the hall.

As I began and remembered the previous day's troubled rehearsal I now felt that the piece would be OK and hoped that the Australian audience would be fair in their hearing of it, should they be as unfamiliar with twentieth century music as was the orchestra. As I walked I was enjoying the beautiful early evening with a light wind rustling through the trees above. I could hear, a short distance ahead, cars and people arriving at the concert hall.

Just then, I yelled as I felt a sharp pain on my head. An enormous fruit bat had swooped down from nowhere, taking with it what felt like a sizable chunk of me. I felt blood coming out of my head as my attacker was in the process of making a full turn for another dive. Now running down the path, the bat took another dive toward me. That did it. I broke off a reasonable limb from a bush and thought, if it's a fight he wants, so be it. As I ran clenching my weapon, sure enough, a fight he wanted. I gave it my best shot but not enough to discourage it. By now, with the creature still rampaging straight toward me, every old Bella Lagossi vampire movie I'd seen was in mind, with those hokey-looking, wooden winged bats that seemed to be suspended on strings. But to my absolute terror, the bat flying after me looked exactly the same.

Now pure fear took over as my adrenaline skyrocketed. I didn't take another swipe because I was too busy outrunning it. When I arrived at the back door of the concert hall, I was soaked through with perspiration, holding the top of my head so as not to bleed all over my white dress shirt. Thoroughly out of breath and unable to explain to anybody what had happened, I made what must have looked like a walking stampede toward my dressing room. The backstage gossip was that I was in some sort of pathological state, the probable result of our previous day's rehearsal, not to mention my assumed anxiety over a nationally broadcast performance of the Australian Premiere of the Barber Piano Concerto.

When I had finished mopping up and began with shaking hands to tie my tie (a minor feat that can be deceivingly annoying under even calm circumstances), there was a timid knock at my dressing room door. Busy in mid tie, I simply said, "Come in", without turning around. As the conductor and the orchestra manager walked meekly into my room, they were all but on their knees expressing their contrition about the previous day's difficulties.

There was no way I could adequately explain that my state had absolutely nothing to do with what for which they were atoning. However, I have to admit that an apology of this sort from a conductor is so rare in any soloist's life that all I could bring myself to say was, "Thank you."

Just before we walked out for the Barber, I told the conductor warmly that I was sure the performance would be just fine. He nodded with a broad smile as we went out to what became quite a little triumph for all of us, including Mr. Barber.

At intermission the four drunk Texans arrived in my dressing room in an even greater state of enthusiasm than before. The conductor and the orchestra manager also came in, and I introduced them all. As the object of this noisy Texan adulation, I began to feel a little bit like a real celebrity, so I seized the opportunity to suggest that we find a place afterwards and all do a little bit of real Texan-style celebrating. The loudest Texan took it upon himself to go find a restaurant that would cater even to us.

After we had all settled over a couple of bottles of champagne, ordered dinner, and a quiet moment at hand, I had the pleasure of telling all of my new friends, the conductor and manager about my fracas with the fruit bat. Nearing the end of my story, the conductor rose half out of his seat, eyes bulging with a bit of justified indignation and nearly choking with laughter, " . . . and you let me grovel to you like that in your dressing room, letting me think this and think that . . . " After having been allowed to suffer as long as possible, to his credit, we all had a good laugh.

Oh yes, the trombone players, secretly confident of an overnight mastery of 5/8 time, took matters into their own hands by returning to the original quarter note plus three eighth notes in the tune of the last movement. The recording of their 6/8 lilting miraculously against everyone else's 5/8 remains a treasure in my recording library. Mr. Barber nearly died laughing when he heard it.

———⋅———

About mid tour the airline (the one and only run by the government) went on strike. I was offered the choice to cancel the affected concerts, retaining my fees, but having survived my illness back in Sydney, this didn't seem such an obstacle. Accompanied by a representative of the ABC, we headed north in an old government-supplied DC3 toward the sugarcane country and cities near the Great Barrier Reef.

In a country where most women remain homemakers and full-time moms, and in which government control of wages enables a young man working as a waiter to comfortably provide for an average family and even own a home, one doesn't encounter as many women in important professional positions as in the United States. In fairness, we have paid a price in America for woman's rightful position in the workplace. Similar as our two countries are, there's an important difference, especially in Australia's young adult men, whose easy social grace and broad cultural knowledge and curiosity suggest an upbringing influenced by a full-time mother.

If Australia is a 'man's world,' the good spirits and easy camaraderie of its men seemed to me in surprising contrast to expressions of resentment expressed by the opposite sex, sometimes frustrated by lingering attitudes that a woman's place is simply in the home. Rather than complain, my traveling companion was the exception, balancing a husband and child with a good position in the ABC. Jenny's love of life and professional savvy transformed what would have been simply an obligation into a fun adventure. Just moments after our meeting I was thoroughly distracted from her good looks to find myself in a gleeful huddle planning the means of our mutual sanity. For two and a half weeks in a noisy, slow DC3 as both home and transport, Jenny was a gift from heaven—a manager, a domestic and secretary—if sometimes a boss.

Arriving in the northern city of Cairns, I began to inquire about fishing or sightseeing out on the Great Barrier Reef. A few days later and a few towns south would provide the best chance for an excursion. Jenny had arranged a quick trip, some 70 miles east of MacKay to a small lagoon adjacent to a tiny island on which we were joined by a teenage boy and his grandfather. With a concert that same night, we got an early morning start in a small seaplane.

As we approached we circled several times, watching large sharks and rays fleeing over the edges of the bowl-shaped lagoon as the final moments of the declining tide called a halt to mealtime. As the last fled, we put down right in our own private paradise and were lectured on animals that could sting, bite, or were poisonous—a rather long list. However, any trepidation vanished as we slipped into a world of mesmerizing beauty and wonder for which no amount of time would suffice. All too soon, with the mainland about seventy miles away and in need of a meal before an eight-o-clock concert, we'd barely make it.

As we returned to MacKay we passed over the town toward the little airport we'd left early that morning. During our final descent, a strange tone seemed to come into the conversation between pilot and tower. Straining to decipher thick Aussie accents through a scratchy radio and the engine noise, as we flew by the tower a second time I was pretty sure things were not kosher.

Even seaplanes have wheels tucked up inside the pontoons. When our second flyby confirmed that ours were failing to lower, my first question was about swinging a few miles back out over the water to set down. No luck. Our frugal pilot had put only as much fuel on board as was absolutely necessary for our trip. Even another circle of the airport would find us running out! The pilot quickly instructed me on what to expect and to do as we would shortly be putting the seaplane down on the runway right on its pontoons.

As the airport just ahead approached he leaned over to me in the co-pilot's seat shouting special instructions: in the event of a fire, the instant we stopped I was to smack the round plate over my chest, releasing the safety belt, then scramble around my seat and fling open the door on the other side of the plane, release Jenny's belt and grab her by whatever means necessary in order to literally throw her out; without an instant's hesitation I was to reach over her seat, release the boy's belt and with both hands, grab his long hair and hoist him headlong, toward and over myself with such force that we'd fly out of the plane together in a heap. In seconds, without regard to discomfort or even injury, I was to get Jenny, the boy and myself out.

"What about the old man?" I yelled.

"Leave him."

As I turned forward the runway ahead was swarming with vehicles rushing toward our target. All I could sense was the bare physical reality of gravity pulling us mercilessly down with the deafening sounds of rushing wind and engine. I felt a horrible choking spasm in my chest and throat as the ground seemed now to rush up towards us as if seizing its own role in our destruction. As if he had practiced a hundred times before, and indeed so, in a hundred of the pilot's nightmares perhaps he had, for after disposing of one then the other pontoon, the plane made a clumsy pirouette as sparks exploded from a wing tip that connected with the runway. After an additional dizzying halfspin, we stopped with a thud.

As I smacked the plate on my chest and began to wheel around I felt a reassuring hand on my forearm. I glanced up to see a faint smile from the pilot.

"It's OK. Take your time." Jenny and I had little time for thanks and goodbyes, for just off the runway was our car and driver nervously pointing at his watch and moving us on.

"My god. I've got to play."

In the car, I discovered my concert clothes and a few bites of food that were assembled when our late arrival became known. Arriving at the hall with no time to spare and barely dressed, Jenny said, "Just one question

Mark... what were you thinking just before we... well, hit?"

I had no idea what Jenny was talking about.

"Thinking? When? What do you mean, Jenny?"

"Don't you remember? What you yelled right before?"

And now smiling as if about to reveal a cherished secret, Jenny methodically began, "Well, after the pilot screamed all those instructions to you, I watched you look straight ahead, take a huge breath of air and lean forward—just looking out with your eyes bulging. Suddenly, just before we hit you lurched bolt upright in your seat, turned your face straight up, and screamed at the top of your lungs, 'NOT YET!'"

For many years I had not flinched from personal sacrifice in the pursuit of my musical goals. I had no difficulty in maintaining reasonable discipline with a daily workout, usually swimming, generally practicing an athlete's Spartan moderation of indulgences as well. During my twenties and early thirties as I grew professionally, the nature of being in the public eye compelled me toward increasing privacy. This, combined with the solitude of relentless practice and constant travel undoubtedly made assessing my basic nature difficult to any but those willing and able to take a second look. It was then my great good fortune to be blessed with the personal attentions and even affections of some who not only supported my artistic quest, but actually sought me out, adding friendship and even intimacy to my young life. Without doubt, this helped to steer me from the eventual maladies of ego-centrism awaiting one whose abilities, sense of purpose, and powers of persuasion made it dangerously possible to live life too much on his own terms.

If talent and brains were the keys to successful relationships, we might more often see people possessing those assets doing measurably better. But with the gifted in mind, I defer to my sister's wisdom: that the problem for intelligent people is that they're always the last to know when they're wrong.

During the years following my pivotal Chicago Symphony performances, as my experience in realms both professional and personal steadily increased, rather than satisfied, I found my appetite for both steadily increasing. As a result, the extraordinary demands of extended tours with long periods away from home forced me to face my limits, examine my true needs and search for a successful balance. A couple of years later, toward the end of the Australian tour, I began a serious struggle with a growing antipathy.

In Tasmania I was befriended by Father John Wall, a priest of considerable position in those parts. After a pair of concerto performances in Hobart, I was delighted to keep his fine company for a hop across the island for a recital. During some introspection on the subject of long tours, I surprised myself by complaining that what bothered me was not that I missed someone in particular, but that I missed no one in particular. I was beginning to wonder that if I didn't get a grip on my professional drive, over time I would become just as much a visitor to the city in which I lived as any I'd visit to play a concert. Despite my private complaint that too many folks don't differentiate between their lives and their lifestyles, my failing to even consider the issue was bound, if unchecked indefinitely, to make me just as muddled.

I had long before accepted that the prizes one seeks in life come at a price. One presses forward with eyes fully open to this fact while maintaining only one acceptable standard: one's best. If at times in your life when you find yourself either unable or unwilling to do whatever necessary to do the very best you can, or when unfair criticism or a personal slight leads you to reconsider the choices you have made or to envy what others have, smile. Thank yourself for never betraying the love you had within for whatever the goal may have been. Smile, and enjoy the glow of your own gratitude, that which only those who try with all their hearts feel. Enjoy the sense of well-being in simply having done your best, and try to find patience, understanding and even forgiveness for those who live on in smoldering anger—the mean spirited, judgmental, even destructive people who lash out at those with the courage to follow their star.

Remember that the sometimes hurtful deeds of such people are the result not of jealousy, but rather of a desperate effort to deflect the thrust of their anger from its true target: themselves. They sadly remind us that nothing is as painful in retrospect as inaction. Whether mastery of an art, the pursuit of an idea, or committed devotion to a person; whether viewed as worthy by others, or scorned loudly by all—to deny love all one's efforts and all one's ardor is to deny one's self.

Aprés Les Concerts (Pardon My French)

A performer's responsibilities are not completed until having enjoyed, or perhaps survived an obligatory after-concert affair. If not made, some careers have been greatly enhanced by social savvy, quick wit, and sometimes a thick skin. Pianist Leonard Pennario was a fine bridge player with a charming personality. Arthur Rubinstein made a point of asking backstage visitors about their lives and interests. Conductor Leonard Bernstein remembered the names of all backstage personnel. As my social responsibilities grew, I collected jokes and stories, often sharing them with my hosts and their guests into the wee hours.

Amidst a grueling twenty-plus recital tour of British Columbia in a little burg named Kitimat, during my performance my belongings were moved a half-hour out of town to a pair of lovely, old fashioned A-frame houses nestled in a dense forest by a lake. That night one of the few post-concert receptions I've honestly enjoyed roared on until the wee hours. I feasted on smoked salmon, homemade pie and was never to be found more than an arm's distance from a punch bowl full of champagne and fresh strawberries. I was later lead through the snow and bedded down in a cozy loft bed in the adjoining A-frame, sleeping snugly in the company of a warm chimney. For one alone and on the road for weeks at a time, a little hospitality can mean so much.

Unusual *après concert* experiences seemed to happen in the South. There ain't nothin' like a little star-power to compel perfectly normal folk into making complete fools of themselves. As a Texas party began to thin out in the wee hours, I was handed the keys to the hostess's Rolls Royce as she warmly suggested I take her lovely college age daughter for a spin. With the keys she also stuffed quite a wad of cash into my hand, suggesting we not worry about coming in late, or for that matter, at all. Despite my poverty and love for good cars, I had to decline, citing an early morning flight. I thought the matter had dropped; but soon after, with my first sip of a very nice Cognac, mom suggested she and I take advantage of the lovely moonlit night instead. I was beginning to wonder if perhaps this family was totally inbred and desperate to introduce some new blood. I did my best not to hurt her feelings by laughing as I politely declined.

By then, more than ready to leave a den of Sirens, I asked the maid to call me a cab if no one was available to transport me to an airport hotel. Just then the man of the house protested that he wouldn't hear of such a thing, and that he would chauffeur me just as soon as we enjoyed some conversation in his study over a Cuban cigar and more cognac. I merrily accepted the arrangement, feeling not only grateful for the intervention of an angel of mercy, but also a solid obligation preemptive of any further unpaid professional obligations not specified in my contract. My only lingering concern was to remember despite fatigue and alcohol not to inadvertently reveal a couple of little secrets about the women in his household.

Only once, in all the places that I have been a guest, did I experience a situation from which I could not smoothly exit. In my thirties, a well known pianist, whom I had had the pleasure of knowing since age seventeen, invited me to stay at his Beverly Hills home for a stop over on my way to New Zealand. In his company I was proud to be spoken to and treated as a colleague. After a nice afternoon at the Beach Club and a fine dinner, we spent hours reading duets on a fabulous Steinway that had once belonged to the actor Joseph Cotton.

At nearly three in the morning, I pleaded exhaustion and excused myself to my room. Not long after, the first of numerous and increasingly insistent intrusions occurred. At first I assumed too much alcohol and a little indiscretion were to blame; but if I had had a lock on my door, I'd soon have gladly used it. Compliments became demands in exchange for the day as well as past votes in my favor as a jury member in two major competitions I'd won. By then I was well past embarrassed and just as mad as hell. By the second shoving match, I found myself ready to deck him.

Fortunately I managed a quick exit and was walking with two suitcases—lost, cold, and pissed off—down a winding street somewhere above Beverly Hills. A cop stopped and, after a couple of polite questions, kindly took me to the nearest hotel. I remember writing a letter (redone a hundred times) attempting to salvage a friendship from a really ugly incident, but I was never able to send it. I never received one, either.

My mother often warned me with, "The higher up the ladder one climbs, the more one's ass shows." I consistently tried to better my manners and attention to the needs of others not only to spare myself embarrassment, but as part of an effort to secure concert reengagements. To that end, there was no shortage of both good and questionable examples.

José Greco, the great flamenco dancer, told me of a magnificent dinner party held on Sutton Place in New York City following one of his famous Carnegie Hall dance recitals. The hostess, an old friend of Greco's, was a widow who had a long and close friendship with a recently retired school teacher from Queens. Neither the years nor vastly different social realms of their lives had worn away any of their affection.

Like everyone else, the teacher was thrilled to meet the great dancer. But as the hosts' best friend, she was seated next to Greco at the table. On the other side was Gloria Vanderbilt, the prominent socialite and author of a book on etiquette.

During dinner, every time Greco and the school teacher began to enjoy their conversation they were rudely interrupted by Vanderbilt leaning precariously over the teacher's plate, her long dangling earrings practically swilling in the salad as she attempted to capture Greco in a conversation of her own. After several such interruptions, when the school teacher finally reached the end of her well seasoned patience, she lurched upright with a forced smile and engaged Vanderbilt with a biting Queens accent heard by all, "Are you Glooorria Vaaanderbilt?"

Reply: "Yes . . . yes, I am she," with obvious irritation.

"No, no, no. I mean, *the* Glooorria Vaaanderbilt, of Vaaanderbilt . . . ?"

Sighing with exasperation, Vanderbilt replied, "Yes, I am Gloria Vanderbilt, of *the* Vanderbilts."

"No, no, no. I mean, *the* Glooorria Vaaanderbilt, who wrote the book on etiquette?"

Huffy, Vanderbilt blurted out, "I am that Gloria Vanderbilt, for heaven's sakes."

After a short pause the teacher turned heavenward as if looking for divine guidance, "You're eating with my fork."

Audience members might remember an artist and his performance. Sometimes, an artist recalls a specific concert for reasons of his own.

A former teacher said the piece wasn't worth the work. A good friend of mine simply couldn't stand to hear me practice it. Nevertheless, I was bitten by the Rachmaninoff Sonata No. 2 and felt I'd go batty if I didn't learn it. I worked one summer on this big vehicle and even dug up a score of the original version of the work, making some respectful changes to Rachmaninoff's more succinct second version.

Its first performance was in Port Arthur, Texas. Just before the concert, the local high school principal invited me to have dinner with his family. Already stuck, his wife served frozen pizza and Pepsi. Impossible! Delicately, I tried to ask for some cottage cheese or eggs and toast to get me through the massive Beethoven Diabelli Variations, some Poulenc and the Rachmaninoff, without having a sugar fit or just running down like a clock. Without concealing her displeasure, my hostess begrudgingly rustled it up.

I walked onstage, greeted by three thousand people jammed in the high school auditorium, and was further delighted to see a fine old Steinway concert grand, perfect for the Rachmaninoff. When I began the Sonata, I felt as if I had begun a long ride on a roller coaster and all I could do was just hang on. The reaction was overwhelming. My former teacher's jinx was shattered by those lovely Texans. Backstage I had to sit alone in my dressing room for a few minutes before greeting anyone so I could just stop smiling compulsively.

I visited with all my guests, changed my clothes and packed up to leave the hall. Now I was starving from a meager dinner and a big program. However, absolutely no one was hungry nor could stay up late on a 'school night,' and with hurried thanks I was dumped off at my motel like a load of dirty laundry. In desperation I finally struck out by myself determined to eat, to walk, to think, to do anything but sit alone and hungry in my room.

    I wandered through the humid Texas evening down a four-lane road toward a rumored Denny's. It must have been about the only hangout for the locals, because there wasn't an empty seat anywhere, even at the counter. Noticing my famished distress, a middle aged man sitting alone in one of the booths invited me to share his table. A bit scruffy with a week's beard and the work worn clothes of the swing-shift as a longshoreman, he was a bit of a character, but outgoing and much more hospitable than my hosts. We had a fine time. After touching on recent issues and politics, he asked what brought me to town. When I told him that I had just played a piano concert he simply exploded. He raved that I should have been taken out to a fine dinner afterwards and not left to wander alone through the fog to a Denny's. He finished by adding, "Some people ain't got no f—ing class!"

    I wasn't going to disagree with him, as I became increasingly amused by the lecture that followed regarding social responsibilities to the Arts and how to treat an *artiste*, or *any* guest. This man may never have heard a concert in his life, but was alert to the plight of a hungry stranger and fully capable of the basics of hospitality. Oh yes, he bought me a steak dinner.

    Back in my motel room I read, wrote letters, even made a few long-distance calls awakening friends. It's hard to describe the feeling of joy mixed with loneliness that can follow a good concert. Thanks to the company of that longshoreman I collapsed into sleep with a smile on my face. After all, 'class' is where you find it.

Playing With Love

Coming of Age

Before my boost from Solti and the Chicago Symphony, there was a period of several years during which I felt all but jinxed in my efforts toward a viable concert career. Things just seemed to unravel time and time again—sometimes my fault, sometimes just 'the turn of the screw,' but more often I was screwed by empty promises or the absence of ethics. At one point, I was beginning to worry about my well-being from the strain of it all—the do or die, old-school, 'great artist' training: were the ongoing difficulties and pressure that I put myself under making me a bit quirky?

There was no doubt I had spent far too much time alone, slaving over a hot keyboard. I was a bit uptight in groups and meeting strangers by nature. While I was trying to overcome this, other things must have made me appear to some as a mass of contradictions. Even in my late twenties, still with boyish looks and a forthright if not youthful demeanor, some confused my artistic fervor, natural to anyone of drive and talent, for arrogance. I could all but hear them asking, "Why is the kid who looks like a surfer trying to talk as if he were a professional pianist?" My behavior was not wrong for me. I was wrong for their mindset.

Beginning in my thirties however, I began to enjoy the recognition that had long eluded me. Until then, I struggled on a veritable roller coaster of opportunities and disappointments, one that would have squashed the hopes of many long before. The candor and wisdom of a friend, Dan Hoggatt, on dealing with the misunderstandings, disappointments, and downright cruelty of others came to me during a crucial summer in Portland.

Again belly up broke, I was using this hiatus to look into some works that might be an opportunity to make an unusual impact. One I was wrestling with was Beethoven's Diabelli Variations. Neither Serkin,

Brendel or any of a large number of recordings made me feel satisfied with what I felt in my heart was the real potential of this masterpiece. My study of this work, during a carefree summer in my parents' home and in the proximity of a musical friend, was a turning point in my playing, a floundering career, and looking back, in me as well. I rediscovered, day by day, variation by variation, my innate love and near worshipful excitement for great music.

Dan worked as Music Director for a large neighborhood church. Every day I learned a new variation and shared my study and revelations about this mysterious monolith with an equally intrigued friend. I shared dozens of stories about my career efforts with Dan as well, making no secret of some of the difficulties I had faced. Dan helped me to understand that due to my natural gifts, zeal, joy of life, intelligence, and general blessings all around, there would always be people, even close to me, from whom I would need to protect myself—people neither understanding nor often caring about the harm they could do. I had to understand that this was a natural part of being a bit exceptional. Oblivious to my feelings or fears and disregarding my daily slave labor, to these people, the simple fact of my abilities could make me unworthy of even base considerations of common decency.

A hard lesson for a young person of drive and accomplishment is in the very fact of their abilities sometimes inciting thoroughly unjustified and often devastating attacks by persons with issues of neglect to their passions. Too easily one can search himself for personal fault because he has receivied what is in fact totally unjustifiable poor treatment. Learning to protect one's self is part of protecting the gifts God has given you, as one would protect the value and innocence of a child.

Dan talked to me about my own acceptance of both good and bad fortune and a better understanding of the kind of responsibility I would have to learn in order just to live with myself. He talked about how people like me have to maintain a much stricter code of ethics than others—a spiritual thing, something he seemed to understand well. I listened.

He saw that these burdens were the results of gifts and a genuine closeness to The Creator; however, they were also a source of a certain loneliness that I would learn not to fear. I would begin to understand that for me and others like me, our life currency would be that of giving to others and sometimes, even sacrifice. All very noble I thought, but it seemed a bitter pill, even unfair. Nevertheless, there was a rightness I felt in my gut about it that I could not deny.

As I wrestled with these ideas, I needed a tangible way of putting them to use; so I decided that as events in my life that were either unpleasant or unfair would happen, I would make a simple but solemn promise to myself: that no matter what, I'd never do that to anyone. As that promise began to help me in the present, I learned also that pain from unpleasant times in my past could similarly be eased by making the same kind of promise. I think it's the idea behind 'turning the other cheek.' For me it became a way of accepting hardships that had come my way, replacing each by a sense of peace and even well being. I was beginning to mold a different image of myself as I began to feel better, and the very wrongs that I had endured actually became stepping stones toward my own better nature. Before long, I noticed that I was actually happier.

That summer I lived an almost monastic existence, using a bike for transportation, swimming a half mile nearly every day, working in my parents' garden, and studying the scripture according to Beethoven. At summer's end, neither I nor my playing was the same. Soon after, I would play to Leon Fleischer, Sergio Commissiona and later, Mr. Solti. The blessings of each began to quickly bring concerts with fine American orchestras, foreign tours, including my first of Australia, some big national television appearances, and a chance to return for another hearing in New York City, this time under the auspices of the Young Men's and Young Women's Hebrew Association (or 92nd Street Y), which shared with Tully Hall a position second in prestige only to Carnegie Hall.

For that critical recital, I knew I must settle in at least the minds of those willing to listen not the question of my potential as a newcomer, but now, the abilities of a busy young American pianist. This performance would either mark me in the New York Music Community as a kid from Oregon who didn't have the sense to quit, or that for a little less than a decade while I was knocking determinedly on their doors with the support of many fine artists, loads of recitals and nearly forty concerti in my repertoire, five important prizes and wonderful reviews from Timbuktu, the folks of the New York Music Establishment had not just been sleeping at the switch, but snoring loudly.

Against the advice of a few in New York, but supported by many who'd heard me play it and trumpeted by my mother who was generally cautious about such opinions, I programmed the Beethoven 'Diabelli' Variations, followed by the tiny Poulenc Movements Perpetuals, and three whopping works of Liszt (Sonetto 104, Au bord d'Une Source, and Vallée d'Obermann) creating a long dramatic line and a climax magnificent enough to bring even a program beginning with the 'Diabelli' together. As a matter of fact, I remember vividly the climax of that evening's program being the pianissimo section of Vallée, just before the long crescendo to the end.

Three years after my summer in Oregon had passed, I played that particular recital in New York. The day before, after finishing my on-stage practice, I walked over to Fifth Avenue and then into Central Park, turning south toward mid-town to meet friends for dinner and an evening of diversion from the next day's concerns. It was a blustery, sunny, fall afternoon. My life was so different now, and as I wound my way through the park, feeling that special excitement when one is fully ready to do their best, I felt I must surely be the luckiest person alive. If the universe would prove to be a billion times larger than once thought, we were also learning of particles so small that if you could fire just one through six miles of lead, it wouldn't hit even a single lead atom. From one vantage point, the sum of a person's efforts and hopes are so miniscule, so ridiculous by comparison, that they mean little. But from another, they are so enormous as to be truly on the scale of the gods themselves. Is one's life insignificant or all important?

As I walked along, the answer began to swell up within my chest and throat, and my eyes flooded over with tears which ran down my smiling face. Trying not to make a spectacle of myself, I wondered why, when I was so happy, so excited, should I be crying? I just felt so lucky in those moments to be simply who I was, doing what I could do. Even if it were just this one time, I realized that this alone was more than millions of people would even dream of.

I had come to the point in my life at which my worth could not be measured in money, or a career, or recognition, pounds, feet, miles, light years or even the infinitesimally large or small. One's value to oneself is just as much as the quality of that which one loves, as well as the quality of the love itself. From that point on, regardless of the measures of others, the question of my value was in my hands alone.

I felt as if I would burst. All the love of all the people, from my parents, teachers, friends, and even strangers who had given me so much, was a virtual treasure glowing within me—one which I am able to share in the presence of a person willing to listen. Nothing in my past had ever gone so wrong, nor had I ever been so disappointed or angry or rejected. It had all been good. I was just fine, and always had been.

The day after the concert a review came out on the front page of Arts and Leisure in the Sunday New York Times. That review was read all over the world. Almost embarrassingly good, my friends teased me of having schemed a way to write it myself.

I met up with a lady friend and headed to the Upper East Side for a bit of happy-hour celebration. At a trendy little place, we got entangled with another couple and just after introductions the two girls went, in tandem of course, to the ladies room. I was left alone with the other guy to make small talk. He was immaculately groomed and his clothes were a bit too tight-fitting, I think, in an effort to advertise his physique.

He asked what I did. When I replied that I was a concert pianist, he asked almost scoffingly, "Are you any good?"

I paused, not wanting to dignify the question with an answer but finally gave way to the silliness of it all, and said a blunt "Yes" in defeat.

He leaned pointedly forward and said, "Let me rephrase this. Are you rich?"

"No," I replied, brow furrowed in the confusion of a really stupid question.

He leaned away and took a self-assured swill from his drink, "Well . . . then why did you lie to me? If you really were any good, you'd be rich."

As Shelley appeared from the ladies room, I swooped her up and right toward the front door, "I've said both of our 'goodbyes', and I handed that guy a towel to wipe off the scotch and soda I just threw in his face."

Reflections

During my college years and shortly after, when I was entering competitions, there seemed to be a group of less than a half dozen of us who generally ended up in the finals together, fighting it out. One would win here, someone else at the next. We knew each other's strengths and weaknesses. If someone was playing their very best, look out. If for some reason they were not at their best or had a rough first stage, then usually someone else won. Anyone of us could and did prevail.

When Dianna Walsh (Forbes, now) and I were among the finalists in the first Kapell Competition, we were chatting together just before things began. Nervously making small talk, I asked what she would be playing. Dianna was a sweetheart but a tough competitor, with nerves of steel. As she was heading toward the backstage area she looked back over her shoulder and said, "Liszt Sonata, ha." That was just what she could do—the Liszt Sonata, ice-cold, right out of the gate—taking no prisoners.

I would have been left in a heap to contemplate my puny prospects if she hadn't stopped, mid-exit, and asked me what I was playing.

"Ravel, Gaspard de la Nuit," I replied merrily. The Ravel was one of the few large scale works at least as difficult as the Liszt Sonata. What was I so worried about?

We gave each other a hug wishing each other good luck. As Dianna left, I heard her mutter darkly, "Shit."

I won.

There was a joke in musical circles in my hometown that went, "Mark Westcott can make any piece sound like Beethoven." Now mind you, as a young man I played Beethoven, even late Beethoven, very well. As a matter of fact, when I won the first Kapell competition, the 'Hammerklavier' Sonata was on my first stage program. When the joke came my way by way of a friend, I think I really surprised her by not only laughing, but by finding merit in it. I endeavored to broaden my range with more repertoire outside of my comfort zone of Bach, Mozart, Beethoven, Brahms, Schubert—the classic German-Viennese school. The effort was the basis of some noticeable broadening and maturation in my playing. In front of the public, play what you're sure of. But one must always be filling holes, closing gaps.

Nothing brings us to our spiritual, intellectual, and emotional feet like the discovery from new challenges. In the union of mind, heart, and body working as one, our intellect and our feelings are bound to a moment in time by the physical act of doing. Jolted by a feeling of genuine passion, it is in this state that we can sense ourselves in the likeness of the Creator defining our humanity. Like two sides of a coin, one side of passion is a state of tremendous excitement. The other is what Mr. Mannheimer described as 'relaxed concentration.' In the union of these two unlikely opposites one can find wisdom decades before its time, while retaining the joy of childlike wonder to the very end.

When the Guarneri Quartet recorded for the first time with Rubenstein he was already, I believe, in his seventies. They were not only struck by the fire and youthful vitality of his playing, but that of him as well.

A friend of mine who studied at Curtis used to see a grandfatherly Rudolph Serkin bounding up stairs two or three at a time en route to a lesson.

At nearly eighty, when walking behind Mrs. Genhart up the Eastman stairs, one saw the figure of a young woman.

These people and others like them didn't just seem young, they remained young. Despite the mastery acquired early in their lives, due to an insatiable curiosity and genuine humility, they possessed a compulsion to 'look again' at works they'd known and played for as many as fifty years, studying or teaching each anew as if for the very first time. It was assumed there was always a better way. As Mr. Serkin said, "There are no artists versus students—only students at different levels."

Studying a work is a vast and complex series of decisions followed by learning to project them in sound. Along the way one must take a position or point of view. Though important to do with conviction, I believe this is an act of faith more than one of absolute certainty. At its best, this process grows from love—love for the music guided by the sure hand of the genius who composed it. And, like love, this attitude carries just a bit of uncertainty. This is why we say "I love you" more than once. Each time we do, we reaffirm love; but we also redefine it as we grow and change. The words do not lose their meaning by repetition, but gain meaning by the occasion or context in which they are uttered.

The same applies to the artistic pursuit: one strives not only to know but to love—to cherish. For the teacher and performer, another step is added—sharing. One's performing repertoire, that which is brought out in front of the public, is only a portion of what is known. Beneath the surface exists that which can decide whether your playing is that of an artist or an amateur. Surrounding this heard and unheard body of music is the world of art—in fact, the world itself. One's playing is only as broad as one's life. It is also a reflection of one's general emotional, physical, and spiritual state—just like handwriting. With this in mind, living in balance, in moderation, and in good health is of the utmost importance.

In the pursuit of excellence, hard work and diligence is only part of the recipe for success. The many issues of making sound choices and living as we all know we should is the foundation upon which we work. To this end one must learn the difference between being stubborn and being tenacious. While these are similar traits, one has disastrous consequences while the other is invaluable. One must know the difference between diligence and drudgery, imagination and indulgence, and always, always, between one's passions and one's appetites.

Especially during difficult times of heavy practice, meeting deadlines, or working under a lot of pressure, make a point everyday to get away from work and have some fun. Gieseking said that nothing is more important than being fresh. Audiences attend concerts to see and hear an artist, a real performer, not just an accomplished piano player. Find a way. Make the time.

Big artist, big idea. A great performance, just like a great work of music, has a sense that it sprouts from a single idea—one which is present from beginning to end. Projecting this idea throughout the ups and downs of a work can make the difference between playing notes and creating a real performance. It is an idea central to all of the arts.

When I saw the great American ballerina Cynthia Gregory dance Swan Lake, I was reminded that the prince does not fall in love with the first cousin to a duck. Ms. Gregory danced with the large, strong gestures of an anguished woman, not the nervous fluttering of a feathered creature one so often sees in this ballet. Also, all but imperceptibly Gregory kept her torso just a bit forward and her head a bit down for the whole act until the moment the evil sorcerer again transformed her into the swan when she straightened fully upright for the very first time. The effect was that she seemed literally to float, weightlessly dragged toward the sorcerer's menacing grasp. The audience gasped audibly. The effect was staggering. The plan behind it was simple, yet powerful. Big idea.

While at Eastman I attended a performance of Rudolph Nureyev appearing with a big Canadian ballet company. After nearly two hours, the great Russian dancer finally appeared for no more than fifteen minutes of the most tepid dancing imaginable. Rudy's famous cat like feet might just have been nailed to the floor. To their credit, the Rochester audience was only slightly more polite in their response than he in his apparent attitude toward them. When the house lights came up our group was no longer eager to accept an invitation to go backstage.

Years before, in a cold, muddy, stinking little USSR town on the edge of nowhere, a troop of dancers came to dance on a makeshift platform, perhaps paid only by their lodging and food. One of them must have had the heart of a lion and the legs of a gazelle. The infectious joy with which he danced made even the near constant pain a dancer knows all too well disappear, leaving only beauty.

In that audience was a scruffy little boy with a quick temper and an oddly chiseled face, who at that moment felt a lion stir within his own chest. That boy would go miraculously on to become the most celebrated dancer of his time, setting audiences ablaze with leaps that seemed to stop in midair, igniting the stage with a riveting personal intensity, and developing among all male dancers an utterly unique sense of 'legato.'

Mr. Nureyev's contempt for his audience in Rochester was not his greatest sin. In fact, what he did or perhaps did not do demonstrated a contempt for himself by forgetting his roots.

Performing is an act of sharing, ultimately rooted in love. Empowered by love, it can overcome great odds. But over time, also like love, if spurned or neglected, it can slip from grasp, sometimes never to return.

Soon after my arrival in New York, I met the legendary tennis player Bjorn Borg. At that time I was all but overwhelmed by the complexities and pressures I was facing as a young struggling pianist. Over lunch I confessed that I was having trouble with nerves and that I was not playing my best under pressure. As we discussed the pressure of public scrutiny and constant training, Borg told me that when he practiced he imagined that his next match would be against a top rival in top shape, that his racquet would have some bad strings, that he would be sick with a high fever, or perhaps playing on little or no sleep—any number of difficult negative factors. With this in mind, he would practice in a way in which he felt he could guarantee an acceptable bottom line on the court.

We all perform better on some days than others; so many factors are in the mix. I think we do ourselves a favor at the moment we stop believing in having a good or a bad day. I have come to instead rely on the fact that a performance's quality is directly proportional to the quality of preparation. With that in mind, not only can one's practice improve, but one's performances as well as the state of mind with which one faces them.

The CEO of a huge Japanese corporation, and one of the richest men in the world, made an interesting point in an interview for a financial magazine. When asked what attributes he might look for in choosing a new vice president, he surprised the interviewer by answering, "I would look for someone who played piano or violin very, very well." Seeing that the interviewer was more than perplexed, the CEO generously continued, "I am looking for a person who is capable of persuading by means *other* than brute force."

A New Challenge

For over a decade and a half tours had come and gone. Some were wonderful; some were not. In my early forties I tried a couple of short-term university teaching positions, each designed with a heavy concentration on performing for recruitment and fund-raising. Even with the panache and freedom of "artist-in-resident" after five years in each, before too long I clearly understood Henry Kissinger's wry remark: "The reason university politics are so bad is because the stakes are so low." As I was juggling the choice in my future between continuing with the rank of an associate professor or trading some of its inherent security for an in-earnest effort to return to full-time concertizing, I was stopped dead in my tracks.

In the early 90s I noticed a very small but persistent patch of flaky, dry skin on the bridge of my nose. Since adolescence I had been generally free of any skin problems so I took notice as it persevered. When some impatience left a small amount of bleeding as I pulled it free, with no particular alarm I decided to take the matter to a dermatologist.

Until that point in my life I had been generally lucky with medical issues, sparing one or two maladies as a result of touring in foreign countries. Hepatitis set me back a few months, but deepened my appreciation for the color yellow as well as my abhorrence of daytime television. The other, after a short tour in Mexico which ended with a brief vacation in Acapulco, was an intestinal battle of near epic proportions in which I was so suddenly and violently doubled over that just negotiating myself and one article of baggage to the airport and on an airplane home still ranks in memory as among the most difficult hours of my life. I actually landed in a seat not commonly used by paying airline customers, and by that point in the flight, wisely, no one even tried to send me back from the bathroom to my assigned seat, a rare moment when the common good of the many actually prevailed over FAA regulations. A cab took me directly from the airport to the emergency room of the Kaiser Hospital near my home in San Francisco. By just a few words and what must have been my obvious physical state, the nurse on the other side of the glass actually passed a pair of Sulfa tablets and a small paper cup of water through to me as she was taking my vital information. One can't ask for faster treatment than that. I'd connected with a nasty bacteria called Shigella. You don't want it.

Despite these and relatively minor skirmishes, I've been blessed my whole life with an uncommonly strong constitution both in fighting off ailments and recuperative power, as well as counting on high levels of physical energy. These gifts from my parents had been in the front ranks of the demands I faced as a concert artist, but would now see duty to an extent I could never have foreseen in the ways for which they were designed by nature: saving my life. In retrospect there is little doubt that my fair Scandinavian skin and a relentless love for the out-of-doors added greatly to the risk of skin cancer.

Whether due to all of this good fortune, or just my basic nature, I think I was a terrible coward facing things medical. Around forty, following a badly broken left arm from a fall off of a ladder, and facing my first surgery since an all but forgotten childhood tonsillectomy, I requested a short personal conference with the anesthesiologist during which I timidly confessed the overwhelming fear that I'd never reawaken. The doctor kindly confided to me that only months before he had undergone his own first surgery, and to his great surprise and chagrin was just as big a coward as I. As we laughed together, I was better able to face the unknown.

At its beginning, by comparison to these brief but memorable bouts, it seemed that the little patch of stubborn dry skin on my nose was but a trifle. As I waited patiently during a return visit to the dermatologist for the results of my previous appointment's biopsy, I felt no particular trepidation. Even should the results suggest a malignancy, this little patch of dry skin was barely a quarter of an inch in size and hardly seemed to me the kind of acorn from which a mighty medical oak could grow.

As the results were conveyed, all seemed pretty much straightforward: a simple basal cell carcinoma—the kind generally to be taken care of with a minor procedure called Mohs surgery. However, pathology had also detected the faint but troubling evidence of a second cell called squamous. Although the surgical solution for this coexisting cell was part of the same procedure, it raised the stakes considerably.

By comparison the squamous cell is much more dangerous. Like the dreaded melanoma, it can grow very rapidly to threaten surrounding tissue and organs. Like a melanoma, it can be the basis of a cancer invading, through one means or another, the body in general and becoming unwieldy, difficult or impossible to treat, ending in great tissue loss or even death. Unlike the downward dive of a melanoma, a squamous cell crawls horizontally on its belly. Having started in the middle of my face, it endangered my eyes, the structure of my nose, the tissue of my cheeks and, God forbid, even more.

The immediate threats of this unwelcome intruder included not only my face and the extent to which it may have grown undetected, but the extent also to which it might continue to evade the scrutiny of even the most exacting Mohs procedure, still to this day the gold standard from early detection for initial surgical removal of skin cancers. During this procedure, with the patient fully awake but somewhat lethargic and pliable, due usually to the merciful application of a drug like valium, the skin within a perimeter around the lesion is carefully removed. The contours from side to side as well as depth are carefully charted so that under careful microscopic examination any extending malignancy in any direction is cause for another visit to the surgical chair and additional removal of tissue. As little bits of one are unceremoniously cut away, this process of hourly visits is disconcerting at best and, on a location like one's face, darned difficult. Adding to the general stress of the ordeal, beside the uncertainty of awaiting the hourly verdict of each visit, upon every return to the surgical room, additional injections of xylocaine must also be given, most often right in the raw tissue of the previously excised area in order to numb for more removal. I couldn't help but wonder if the shots to block the pain of additional cutting weren't nearly as bad as enduring the cutting itself unaided.

It would have been totally improbable to have gotten through all of this without returning at least once for some more removal of my face. That conclusion I came to long before it became fact, if for no other reason than to spare myself inevitable disappointment. After four and even five returns, I'm sure that the surgeons were just as tired and discouraged as was I.

At the end of a very long day a huge question remained unanswered: How long and how difficult would full elimination of the cancer and the repair of my face actually be? The answer, despite eventual but qualified success, would be: longer and more arduous and costly than I ever could have imagined, lasting a decade with over two dozen surgeries, radiation treatment and the loss of nearly everything in my life which did not exist fully within or physically attached to me. I was in trouble and headed for more.

As I drove home with bandages covering everything but my eyes and mouth, I numbly promised myself not to contemplate the unknown, taking only one uncertain step at a time. At least this way I'd not die of worry.

The initial biopsy's faint trace of that secondary squamous cell was only a hint of its true stature within the epidermal layers of my nose and cheeks. Its removal had exacted a heavy price. How it would ever be repaired I had no clue, but foreseeing the typical rampage of a squamous, the head of dermatology oncology had hoped to spare me a typical half dozen or more surgeries necessary to repair a gaping removal of skin several inches across the middle of my face.

In all, I received superb care throughout the years of treatment at OHSU (Oregon Health and Sciences University). Portland and the whole Northwest is blessed to have this world-class teaching hospital with a medical staff responsible not only for the treatment of patients but the training of young resident doctors as well. This double function assures state-of-the-art knowledge and resources resulting in fine patient care. However, like any professional or university environment, occasional political intrigues can and do occur.

At the time of my big Mohs surgery, a top plastic surgeon practicing in Chicago had developed a remarkable technique to recover large areas of removed facial tissue, as in my case, in just one adroit surgery.

Although expensive, in the long run it provided savings over the normal process called a forehead flap, which usually necessitated a number of follow-up procedures to obtain satisfactory aesthetic results, not to mention the stress and general hardship of a couple of years of surgeries endured by the patient. The head of Dermatology Oncology, Dr. Neil Swanson, who was responsible for the removal stage of my endeavor, with considerable personal effort and the application of some professional pressure, had arranged for me to go to Chicago immediately after the Mohs procedure for this single surgery. The tough part in the equation was neither medical nor coordination between various distant teams of doctors, but in convincing the Oregon Health Plan of the medical and financial wisdom of this strategy.

Early on, just after the initial biopsy and a couple of short semi-conscious surgeries to remove and fix what had seemed just a small problem, I was dropped by my regular medical coverage. Considered from that point to be uninsurable as a result of a single small skin malignancy on the bridge of my nose, my only option was to turn to the Oregon Health Plan. Many in our state are rightly proud of a public health plan for those falling between the cracks of traditional medical coverage. Despite occasional difficulties, I owe the Oregon Health Plan and the people behind its conception no less than my life, and I continue as I can from time to time to do all that I can to promote public support. Perhaps not perfect, it helps many at a time of little or no substantive action toward a solution to what is no less than a national embarrassment. Even to naysayers its underlying philosophy and existence declare loudly to all, "We can do better." It provides a living model and practical step in what is, at the very least, the right direction. In the case of my Chicago surgery, however, the Oregon Health Plan was about to cause a huge problem.

Still in bandages, and all but resembling a mummy from the neck up, I flew to Chicago where I was picked up by a violinist friend and her husband who would be my surrogate family as I faced what would be a big and difficult repair surgery. While arranging the upcoming pre-op appointment, I received a surprising phone call, with vague concerns about the long-arranged coverage by the Oregon Health Plan. To my increasing horror, agitated calls revealed that the firmly confirmed authorization was now suddenly but incredibly unconfirmed. I was now totally set adrift, thousands of miles from home, with half of my face gone, and no way on earth to pay for the surgery to put it all back together.

Struggling for composure I called Dr. Swanson's office at OHSU, and although I do not recall today the complete specifics of the conversation, it's a good chance that I threw a fit. It was in that very dark and frightening hour that I was introduced to a living angel of mercy and the lady who would become a close and valued friend, the patient advocate at OHSU, Barbara Glidewell.

Why this debacle had happened, although an item of angering concern, I would have to wait a bit to discover. With an area several inches across my face laid wide open, with all the discomfort and huge risk of infection and a mental state teetering on the edge of composure, Barbara's first concern was to get me back to OHSU. I was now deftly delivered by Barbara's adroit efforts and soothing tone toward a solution.

During the next day's return flight to Portland, as I drifted in and out of sleep, I could not help but wonder what had gone wrong with all of Dr. Swanson's careful arrangements. For the time being, all I could do was concede to facing perhaps a half dozen surgeries beginning with an arduous forehead flap.

I was picked up in Portland by Barbara Glidewell herself. Although I was more than grateful for her intervention into the affair, somehow it seemed that she may have personally chosen to come to the airport in order to reveal some of the details underlying the retraction of coverage of the Chicago surgery. My suspicions were confirmed as Barbara revealed the findings of twenty-four intense hours of detective work into what had gone very wrong. It was no more nor less than the thoughtless and reckless verbal meanderings of Dr. Swanson's own nurse.

Evidently, she had an old friendship with a gal who worked at the Oregon Health Plan, with whom she often chatted. At the very time Dr. Swanson was campaigning for support of the strategy of the Chicago operation, she had been diligently saying to her friend that she didn't understand why I needed to go to Chicago when there were people right at OHSU who could put my face back together again. With neither knowledge nor understanding of the differences in procedure, in reckless disregard for her own superior's efforts, combined with her brainless babbling and additional contempt for a patient's privacy and well-being, she managed to drop the seed of suspicion into the collective mind of the Oregon Health Plan, who disapproved the surgery the very day I arrived in Chicago.

Whatever Dr. Swanson may or may not have decided to do with his nurse, I asked Barbara to arrange for me the opportunity to see the director of OHSU. Although it would be several weeks until I was fit and ready to do so, when the time came I was provided a full half hour in the man's office, during which I not only pulled no punches but was offered not one single excuse nor argument to my heated indignation. The man could not have enjoyed those thirty minutes, but I'm sure my tongue-lashing was a darned sight better than the lawsuit I might have rightfully contemplated. The fact was that although the nurse's behavior was inept, reckless, and ultimately unprofessional, I could not honestly claim to have been extensively damaged by the results of her actions. What I was after at this time was not money, but rather peace of mind, perhaps a little closure, and a bit of personal satisfaction.

The forehead flap is an amazing surgery. A triangle taken from above the nose and between the eyebrows, up and broadly across the forehead, is used to recover the middle of the face, in my case the surface of the nose and the large area across both cheeks. Skin is enormously elastic, a quality which makes this operation ultimately possible. The big issue is providing a blood supply to the graft for good healing by preserving the large vein running up above the nose vertically to the forehead, the one people often see when one gets angry. The large, broad triangle of skin is removed, while leaving the lower portion nourished by the vein attached. The whole triangle is then flipped down and across the middle of the face with its own attached blood supply, now above and protruding a full inch or so beyond the face. This pedicle makes this procedure successful by providing a reliable blood supply to a large area until enough vascular structure has developed enabling it to survive independently.

For ten days after surgery the patient must change a small bit of dressing lodged between the pedicle and the forehead so that it does not start growing closed. The pedicle is then removed, a welcome bit of secondary surgery after which one no longer feels as though he had a vegetable growing out from between his eyes.

The part of the forehead flap surgery that makes it so painful afterwards results from the closure of the area from which the resurfacing triangle is taken. With the natural elasticity of skin very much in play, success is achieved by some clever piecing together of the area and a great deal of pulling and stretching. One unexpected plus is the free face lift obtained in the process. Despite the fact that one may look for some time very much like a creation of Frankenstein, with scars going every which way, one can at least take a certain solace in looking like a young Frankenstein.

Of all the surgeries that I endured over these years the post-operative pain I endured after this particular surgery was almost more than I could bear. I awakened after surgery throwing up violently, a persistent symptom characteristically following deep general anesthesia. Adding to the ordeal was a tight, heavy elastic turban holding me all together. Like a pair of gigantic hands pressing with full might on all sides of my skull and forehead, inside was the large area for which the recovering tissue had been taken and then forcibly closed. The combination of general post-surgical pain from all the cutting and sewing, the inevitable swelling and the tremendous pressure exerted by the turban was no less than agonizing. On top of that, every time I moved a muscle, I threw up again, sending the blood pressure in my head sky high and making the pain even worse, if that were possible. Eventually I was on a hefty dose of post-surgical medication and managed, with both nausea and pain under control, to catch bits of sleep.

The forehead flap was the first of several surgeries that I would undergo in getting my face from scary to almost OK. Throughout this process, particularly when I was stuck for a matter of days with large areas of open tissue, I developed the dexterity of a blind person, refusing, or perhaps simply unable to look into a mirror at the carnage. I laugh about it now, but it was not funny at the time. I just couldn't look. Nevertheless, over many surgeries I changed countless dressings, cleaned many areas of tissue, and never had a problem with infection or healing. I'm not sure that facing all of life's issues dead-on is always the very best tactic.

The forehead flap also was my introduction to a magnificent plastic surgeon and a fine fellow by the name of Dr. Ted Cook. At our first meeting, upon my return from Chicago, I realized in short order that I was in the presence of a true egomaniac—in the very best sense. Reminding me of some of the better conductors with whom I have played, Ted's was the kind of relentless professional pride and confidence that both assumes respect and provides immediate assurance that the outcome will be a good one.

The next several surgeries were not easy, but I accepted them without question and would eventually come to a point where the results spoke for themselves—they were excellent. Somewhere at about the halfway point I found myself in day surgery being prepped yet again. I had become accustomed to a certain caring and affable treatment from all parts of the surgical staff, from those dark early morning check-ins and the first girl who carefully fixed an IV in my wrist or forearm, the trip upstairs to pre-op, and my introduction to the day's anesthesiologist under whose care I would remain until that mysterious moment in which I would reawaken. Most often I was taken still awake into the operating room because this made it much easier to be transferred onto the table for surgery. Some people just can't do this, and to be honest, I suppose an operating room is rather scary looking, particularly when one is at the center of attention. What I found most disconcerting was the freezing cold, an obvious necessity for the prevention of infection.

On this particular day, due to the poor attitude of an anesthetic nurse, a mishap occurred which ended up doing me a significant favor. As I was wheeled into pre-op and introduced to this anesthetic nurse, I had not yet had an IV put in. After she drove what looked like a three-penny nail into my wrist, I complained that it was unusually uncomfortable, a remark tersely shrugged off as I was wheeled toward surgery. Although her attitude seemed uncharacteristic of the caring manner to which I had become accustomed, I figured that I would shortly be asleep anyway.

Remembering being wheeled into surgery, my next memory of the day's events was an unlikely but important second glimpse of the interior of the operating room. As on other days, I had been wheeled in and transferred myself onto the table prior to being put asleep. But on this day, I awakened during surgery, looking up to see Dr. Cook's startled associate, Dr. Wong, as he was busily sewing on my face. Next I remember a lot of swearing in Chinese before returning to sleep.

When I reawakened, this time in the right room, that three-penny nail in my wrist was really causing problems, to the point that I was actually concerned about my wrist—no minor consideration for a concert pianist. It hurt like hell, and now I was not only miffed about it but wondering as well about waking up in surgery. I called for a nurse and complained about the IV, asking her to take it out immediately. As she began to tell me that it would have to stay in a little while longer, she glanced down in horror at the size of the spear which had been driven into me. At that point she confirmed my ire about the anesthetic nurse's attitude, commenting that she must have been too lazy to walk all of fifty feet to the hallway closet in order to find the right needle. She took it out immediately.

The next day in Dr. Cook's office, as he was examining Dr. Wong's handiwork, I went calmly but deliberately into the episode of waking up during surgery, as well as the issue of the IV and the surly attitude of the anesthetic nurse. Dr. Cook told me that he would look into the matter. The next day I got a call from him. It seemed that the nurse's attitude in not bothering to find the proper needle reflected a similarly poor general attitude which later resulted in the more serious issue of me awakening during the procedure.

Toward the end of the surgery, as she was called to prepare another patient, I was handed over to her assisting nurse. As I was now learning, right on the cover of my surgical record in the largest possible print are words to the effect of *This patient metabolizes anesthesia three times faster than his weight would suggest*. She failed to convey this important caution while handing me over to the assisting nurse, resulting in me awakening while in surgery. This was no mere accident. As far as Dr. Cook and I were concerned, the kind of attitude demonstrated by the anesthetic nurse in pre-op had resulted in an unacceptable situation while I was at my most helpless. I would not have wanted to be at the receiving end of Dr. Cook's fury, but furious he was.

With the Chicago mess still fresh in mind, this latest bit of nurse nonsense moved me to insist that future surgical procedures all be attended by an anesthesiologist—a doctor, not just an anesthetic nurse. I wasn't about to wait quietly by for strike three, and fortunately, neither Dr. Cook nor Barbara Glidewell saw my position as unreasonable. I had already gone through plenty; who knew how much more I would face, even under the best circumstances.

Dr. Cook arranged the next, and as it would turn out, all the remaining anesthesia work to be done by no less than the head of the department. Before long the radically better results of this change provided firm lessons regarding the range of quality of treatment available to any surgical patient. No longer would I be nauseous, depressed, nor in as much pain awakening from surgery. In fact, the long-term, post-op medication strategies I received from then on actually greatly reduced pain for up to three days following. Never more would I risk missing the next day's important follow-up appointment as a result of being too ill or otherwise physically unable to drive myself across town to the hospital.

From this time forward I can't even remember awakening from anesthesia anywhere other than the room in which I was prepped early in the morning. Never again, even following some deep general anesthesiaes, would I come to in the stark post-operative ward to be confronted by the loud demands of a sergeant-like nurse insisting that I pee on command—no small feat for any semi-conscious fellow, whether by nature a bit pee-shy or not. Barely able to recall one's name, in great pain, struggling for basic composure and utterly helpless, such sternly repeated marching orders present a daunting challenge. Almost never demanded by anyone but a member of the other sex, and also making this feat as improbable as screwing a rolling doughnut, are the accompanying threats that in the case of failure, a catheter will be jammed up the remains of what used to be a reliable friend. All this may perhaps have been in the cause of restoring kidney function, but now, due to this simple but important changeover to a full-fledged anesthesiologist, all this unpleasantness ceased.

I strongly suggest, when facing a surgery, one should use only a full-fledged anesthesiologist—a doctor, not an anesthetist, anesthetic nurse, nor assistant of any kind. You are the number-one advocate for a successful and tolerable experience. Ask good questions, listen well and respectfully to the professionals at hand, but leave no doubt as to your role in the equation nor to your expectation to receive the full benefits of the anesthesiologist's art.

The lingering question following any of these 'fix-up' procedures was if healing alone would bring an acceptable level of success, or would another surgery be needed. Adding to my general reluctance of doing more than reasonable results would demand were other issues between surgeries, such as kenalog injections in my face to reduce swelling and promote a faster return to normal contours. Already less than keen about being poked any and everywhere, I started to feel as if every clinic visit provided a golden opportunity in finding a new and more improbable place in which to drive a needle.

Some years prior, a single but memorable procedure to remove a stubbornly thrombosing hemorrhoid provided what was to become only Number 2 in my big list of horrible shots. Not only was there a sharp, piercing pain, instantly making my eyes water, but more memorable was the sudden bit of involuntary choreography as the machine resembling an expensive stair climber onto which I had unwittingly stepped thrust my half-naked (from the waist-down) body literally 'can over keester'— all in the presence of a particularly pretty nurse.

Dr. Cook warned me that the kenalog injections would hurt. Perhaps his warning was unnecessary with the sight of a very long needle approaching my face. On that particular day a visiting Russian doctor was observing all of Dr. Cook's activities. Somehow I managed a respectable composure and, although perspiring profusely, by the end of the shots had managed to stay silent. As Dr. Cook patted me on the shoulder and filed out, the Russian doctor stopped to shake my hand and said, "Tough guy." If he only knew . . .

For those actually enjoying this, and as long as I am on the subject, the most awful shot I've endured was a needle biopsy of the gland on the side of my neck which was suspiciously enlarged at the time of my bad facial biopsy. Seeing my obvious reluctance about the insertion of a huge needle just below my right ear, the attending doctor emphatically told me that it wouldn't hurt. "No more than a blood test," he said. With that he instructed a good-sized nurse to hold on to me. When his so-called blood test felt as if it had been performed by Dracula's own fangs, I came close to belting him—not due to the pain, but due to being lied to.

If our relationship hadn't already been strained enough, when the gland proved to be in all ways benign, he insisted on taking it out anyway. Why then was a painful pre-operative biopsy necessary? Despite my protest over what I viewed as an unnecessary procedure, compared to the big facial surgery I was then facing, removing this gland for the sake of a little added safety was not unreasonable. I reluctantly complied, although unable to conceal my lingering opinion that this particular doctor was a real jerk.

Strange side effects can result from the unforeseen results of two-dozen surgeries. Some, for which I continue to this day to take a bit of medication, are easily manageable. Others, like the radical change in my appearance, must somehow be accepted over time. But a few that were just darned peculiar may be worthy of mention.

Following big reconstructive procedures, in which lots of tissue was moved around, I experienced the amazing ability of the nervous system and brain to reorganize or reprogram. For some weeks after the forehead flap, when I touched the recovered tip of my nose, I felt the sensation on my forehead. Then suddenly, with little or no warning, touching the same place felt like my nose again.

After the surgery on the gland from my neck, I noticed that from time to time my neck would become very wet. I learned that although the removed gland had been a part of the saliva system, the surrounding nerves that had once stimulated it over the anticipation or taste of food were still intact. Still today, with only sweat glands remaining in the area and the nerves still firing their mealtime messages, somewhat like Pavlov's dog, anticipating good food, I get a wet neck.

A more grotesque result from all the sewing on my face and forehead had to do with a large area right at my hairline above the middle of my forehead which began to swell, raising up over a quarter of an inch and spreading out over a few inches in diameter. When it began to redden and develop some sensitivity, it also developed an ugly pit—one large enough to put the eraser end of a pencil fully into. During my visit to

Dr. Cook's resident, I learned that this hole was the kind of ulceration which often develops where skin containing hair follicles has been folded together and closed. Under these circumstances the body often reacts to the buried hair which continues to grow as it would a foreign substance, thus the ulcer forms.

When the young doctor told me there was no suitable procedure to correct the situation, I reacted with a combination of disbelief and indignation. The hole had to go. That night I decided to apply some good old-fashioned nursing and see what I could do myself. I carefully sterilized the best pair of tweezers I could find and cleaned the area. Then I took a stiff drink and went quietly to work. Soon I was pulling hairs several inches in length and coated with smelly goo from the pit over my forehead. When the sink below was covered in a web of gucky, long hairs I cleaned up, applied an appropriate bandage and went to bed. By the next morning, the area returned to normal and the deep ugly pit at its center nearly gone. This simple, common-sense solution must have been beneath the surgeon's considerations.

As the surgeries came to an end, due to Dr. Cook's wizardry and the efforts of a cooperative and strong patient the results were excellent. After an additional year of healing, my face returned to a close resemblance of its former contours and the scars incurred toward that end dissipated to all but unnoticeable. Years of surgeries interspersed with periods of many months of healing had been the medical prison in which I had lived.

Prior to all this, for over two decades I had been so fully devoted to the traveling life and intense practice solitude of an aspiring pianist that my few friends were spread all over the country. As my career dwindled inevitably away, so too did my friends around the country seem steadily to lose both artistic and personal interest in me. Now, in the fight of my life, living primarily off my dwindling resources in the family home back in Portland, I had few if any friends near at hand.

Until this battle, Portland had been my personal sanctuary. It had been a place to which I could return for the love and support of my parents, to lick my wounds or gather up strength and prepare for a difficult musical challenge, to rest and revisit the natural splendor of the Oregon woods and coast, my personal cathedral and the place in which I have always felt closest to God. When I prayed, I prayed most often as an expression of gratitude for my survival. It didn't occur to me to ask for any special help, because I felt as though I was getting so much already, just by surviving.

Despite dwindling professional activity, I began intuitively to cling to long-forged habits of daily practice, spending hours every day learning new works and digging through masses of unknown repertoire. To that end I researched books on music for the piano, filling out stacks of inter-library loan requests as well as perusing the huge library of lesser-known works left to me by Aurora Underwood. Despite long periods of little or no public performances, during these difficult years I did some of the best playing of my life—most of which went unheard by anyone but me.

As the surgeries ground on, I clung to the activities in my life I simply enjoyed to create a lifeline to pull me through the ordeal. Fighting the cancer had compromised the artistic and career goals in my life that I had worked toward for so many years. It was now my return to the little things in life—many of which I had set aside for far too long, sacrificed in favor of many years of hard work in pursuit of a concert career—but with which I could still connect. These would play a special role in my survival. During these tough years I was often sustained by the joy of walking a stream, fishing pole in hand, the companionship of my dog Kypp, and my enthusiasm for gardening—climaxing when I won Best in Show in the annual and prestigious Oregon Chrysanthemum Society Show.

Despite being unable to perform, simply able to continue my work as a pianist, combined with daily enjoyment of my interests and hobbies, helped me to find enjoyment in every day and feel grateful just to be alive. If the tribute I would pay for that survival was destined to be all that I was now losing, painful as that might be, so be it.

I simply found it healthier to count my blessings than to mourn my losses, and without further delay, directed my best efforts toward a lagging career. This would involve by necessity much waiting, with engagements usually being a year or more down the line. With no clear path ahead, I felt the best strategy was to put faith into daily action by subscribing to Mr. Mannheimer's maxim: "Preparation is the key to opportunity." I began to practice long hours.

The two-car garage at my family home was an unfinished boxy structure separate from the house, located in the very middle of the block. With only minor alterations, its wood structure—with the addition of insulation—would make an excellent studio space for long hours of practice and teaching activities. In it I could put my piano, music library, stereo equipment, library, and all related tools and materials. With an interior space of 20x20 and overhead beams for a high, shed-type ceiling, its acoustics would be OK even if I covered the bare cement with carpet.

Still in bandages I threw myself into creating the workspace I had always wanted but never had time to put together: a real studio, comfortable and soundproof enough for practice at any hour of the day or night. I began by removing the huge 15' wooden door, a tricky feat in handling many hundreds of pounds alone. I used its 2x4s to divide the gaping space it left behind, preparing the way for a 72" glass window and door on one side and a new insulated single garage door on the other.

With the help of a friend's practical electronic knowledge, we spliced some heavy-gauge wire into the main source and ran it over and around for lighting and electrical needs. I created a large space for a picture window looking out into the backyard garden to the east. Then we insulated all around. With the help of another friend I learned about the trials and tribulations of sheet rock, but eventually, and with reasonable results, walls and a ceiling were added. With scrap wood I made a nice oversized sill for the installed window and added other molding and trim.

Finally, the walls and ceiling were painted, and the floor was padded and carpeted wall to wall. This would prove to be the cheapest, quickest, and easiest solution, even if it didn't provide the acoustical results I would have liked. To that end, I constructed a shallow platform on which the piano would be placed from flooring samples from a nearby store. I paid no attention to the slight slant of the floor. With my decision to keep a garage door in the structure, with very little effort the space could be returned to a functioning garage only by lifting the carpet.

In just a couple of months, learning as I went, for very little I had transformed an unfinished garage into a fine studio. Upon seeing the results of my efforts, a well-to-do friend in Southern Oregon obtained estimates from small construction companies for a similar project. They were all between twenty-five and thirty thousand dollars. Besides the personal pride and the very real therapy the project had brought to me, I was also learning why Home Depot is alive and well.

A Return

Having endured about a dozen surgeries, and with Dr. Cook's amazing results in the reconstruction of my face, feeling great and looking surprisingly unscathed, I saw no reason why I shouldn't attempt a full return to playing concerts. An unexpected opportunity came my way when I got a call from the wonderful violinist Sherry Kloss. A conductor with whom I had often played was also one of her first violin teachers years before she would go on to the legendary Jascha Heifetz and distinguish herself by becoming his personal assistant for several years.

After a meeting in Ashland, Oregon, during which we read some duo repertoire, it was clear that we had the making of a good team. On the spot we formed a duo and began planning the long process of choosing, rehearsing and arranging concerts in tandem. As a result of our previous musical histories, we were able to share connections with previous solo concerts and begin a schedule of appearances as a duo.

Perhaps the most wonderful opportunity Sherry brought my way was with our invitation to perform at the Monterey Mozart Festival. In Monterey I was surrounded by such a high artistic level that in short order I nearly felt as if I were fully back in the professional saddle. Conducted by the wonderful Oleg Kovalenko, that ensemble, made up of soloists, concert masters and section leaders from orchestras around the country, was breathtaking. My participation was a personal and professional boost I will always cherish. I returned the following four seasons as featured pianist until the unfortunate demise of this wonderful summer music festival.

Yearly visits to Monterey, like all the concert activities of the next years, became increasingly difficult due to the events that began during the very first return trip home. Driving north toward Portland I stopped in San Francisco to see some old friends and to take, for the first time in a long time, a voluntary vacation. I stopped by the offices of a doctor friend who was a dermatologist. As he was finishing up with patients before our lunch together I used the small office restroom. Glancing at myself in the mirror, illuminated by the soft but penetrating gray-white light of a frosted window, I felt genuinely pleased to soon show him the excellent results of the combined efforts of the OHSU doctors. In the same instant I noticed a peculiar marble-like coloration just below the thin, almost transparent, outer layer of skin. In the unusual light I saw a strange underlying discoloration across the whole middle of my face that was immediately disconcerting. My heart took a jump, despite my private calming efforts to relegate the observation to a bit of oversensitivity. As I looked a second, and then a third time, I blinked in amazement, unable to deny what I was seeing. After a few cordial minutes, I brought the matter up to Jim who took a careful look, probably more out of politeness than real genuine concern, trying to reassure me that all was OK, and that I was probably suffering a bit of natural apprehension.

Still en route to Portland I decided to call Dr. Swanson's office and arrange a biopsy immediately upon arrival. There was just too much at stake to wait even a second, and I would rather look a bit foolish than take any risk. When I was told that I'd have to wait a full two weeks for an appointment, I took matters in hand and went to the private office of a dermatologist I had met socially.

The next day he added his voice to the chorus of others insisting that I was being hyper-sensitive. After all, how would it seem to a doctor to have a patient coming in, all bent out of shape, claiming to see with the aid of some special light, that which only medical professionals can see with the use of a microscope and many years of training? Nevertheless, at this point I knew every detail of my face better than I ever would have wished. I insisted. Begrudgingly he took a small piece from my nose and assured me of the results within twenty-four hours. That night I headed to Vancouver, BC, for a bit of private teaching, which I did for several days every month.

The next day in the middle of a lesson, the doctor called, profoundly apologetic. Unfortunately I was more than right, with the tissue showing substantial squamous presence. He told me with a second apology that he would never again argue with a patient over this kind of matter and took it upon himself to call Dr. Swanson at OHSU to make all arrangements for an immediate Mohs surgery. My remaining lessons were canceled and I was soon in the car en route to Portland where the next morning I would be at it again.

If I could have sent my face to the hospital and somehow pulled the covers over what remained of me, staying safely at home in the very bedroom in which I grew up, I would have gladly done so. Somehow I found the courage to drive across town in the dark early morning hours to meet the unknown. Having displaced a number of other patients, I was whisked into the surgical room and prepped.

Dr. Swanson had been scheduled that morning to give the keynote address at a national conference in Chicago, but upon receiving word of my situation, he kindly stayed to perform the first major part of the process. I would then be handed over for any additional removal of tissue to a pair of younger but, in his words, "brilliant" resident doctors. One was Asian in background, the other with a sophisticated English accent.

The first process was long and arduous with a great deal of tissue taken. In bandages I managed to eat some breakfast in the hospital cafeteria. When I returned to the area the staff was already waiting anxiously for me. I could tell by the grim attempts to keep my spirits up that a lot more cutting was coming. At this point I started receiving injections of xylocaine all over my face in the areas where tissue had been removed and where they would need to take more. The pain was excruciating, and for the first and fortunately only time, I simply lost it. Wherever that particular line in my own constitution was, at that moment, with all the prior ordeal and success now only so much history, I hit bottom.

Dr. Swanson was well on his way to Chicago, and I was in the care of his two fine assistants. Tears were rolling down the side of my face, and my chest was shaking as I quietly sobbed. The young Asian fellow nudged my arm firmly saying, "Now, buck up, Mr. Westcott." As I paid him little attention, thinking that there was a considerable gulf between his skill as a doctor and his skill as a human being, the other fellow quickly admonished him saying, "You are excused. Leave the room, and do not come back until I call for you."

He turned down the surgical lights, only leaving a warm glow in the room, raised the position of my chair until I sat a bit more upright, and quietly slipped one hand under my head while taking my hands in the other. He pressed himself gently against the side of my arm and began talking to me with encouraging warmth. "Everyone in the area has spoken to me about your history with so much admiration and so much affection." As I sat quietly crying in his care, he continued, "I read your chart last night, and it's almost unbelievable what you've been through already. We're not going to go on today until you are entirely ready, no matter how long it takes. We'll just stay here until you feel better." Over the next twenty minutes or so we talked quietly as I regained my composure.

The day did grind on with several more visits to the chair, none of which I remember. What I do remember is that young man and having been tenderly but firmly rescued by his compassion.

This Mohs procedure represented a whole new series of surgeries, the remainder of which would be done under general anesthesia. Before, there had been a wait of a week or more before the recovering process with the forehead flap began. But this time, that procedure came the very next day, the reasons for which were not at this point clear.

Scheduling any of these affairs at a major facility like OHSU is a juggling act under normal circumstances. That only forty-eight hours after a biopsy I should be in the Mohs procedure and only twenty-four hours later on the table for a big surgery was very unusual. A great deal of ordinary procedures must have been altered in order for this to happen, but by design I was on the fast track, as soon as I could be adequately healed, toward radiation therapy and a last ditch effort to put a stop to the rampaging squamous which had deftly undone the surgeon's handiwork, and with it my life in general.

I had not been told that I was going to undergo another forehead flap, probably for good reason. I belong to a very small club of less than two-dozen people in the state of Oregon having had two forehead flaps. Not surprisingly, there was some apprehension about the second due to the fact that this time there would be so little tissue with which to work.

Now, due to the earlier mishap in which I awoke during surgery, my anesthesia for this and all the remaining surgeries was handled by the doctor at the head of the department. Despite the difficulty of covering a large area with little tissue, this forehead flap was considerably better for me. I don't know what that doctor had up his sleeve, but I not only awoke comfortably in the room in which I had started the morning journey, but was without significant pain and eager to go home. I felt so good that on the way home I asked to stop by a grocery store for a few post-surgical favors. When over a half hour had passed, the manager had to be summoned in order to find me, as I was still merrily shopping. What a difference—one which remained the standard for three full days.

Still on the fast track, other surgeries for aesthetic improvement on the basic forehead flap would have to be tackled after radiation therapy. We could not wait a moment, or that darned squamous could gain a foothold again. The reason that bombarding cells with radiation effectively alleviates cancer is that unlike a healthy, normal cell, when subjected to the effects of radiation, a cancer cell does not possess the proper DNA to reproduce. The same irregularity of DNA that makes a malignancy dangerous and uncooperative with its place and function in the body also leads under these conditions to its demise.

I soon began treatment directly to my face, which continued for several weeks. At about the middle of the regime, I began to feel the normal side effects of fatigue, pain, and nausea. A special effort was made to protect my teeth, but alas, despite its success in permanently alleviating the cancer, a few years down the line, after all the remaining surgeries, I would pay for the success of the radiation therapy with the loss of all my teeth.

For some inexplicable reason, this summer and fall had a veritable log-jam of obligations, none of which I really wanted to drop. Facing two months of radiation therapy, my reaction was to curtail all of my musical activities. But I realized that it would be better to curtail just about everything else, find ways to adapt my practice to suit my physical limits, and maintain what was a hefty list of commitments. Frankly, I was scared of allowing a pattern of canceling, should my health difficulties continue. Faced with a gargantuan juggling act and limited energy, exactly how I would do all of this depended on many things. The idea in the solution went back to a saying Mrs. Underwood often used when tackling a difficult or complex work: "Make a plan and stick to it."

Plan or no plan, I would have a great deal with which to contend. During the two months of the radiation treatment I would also be flying to Vancouver, Canada, for long weekends with my summer classes. Less than two weeks after my last treatment, I was engaged to perform a recital program including the hugely difficult Chausson Concerto for Violin, Piano and String Quartet; only one week after, the Beethoven 4th Piano Concerto at a summer music festival; two weeks later I would spend a full week in the recording studio with violinist Sherry Kloss, sweating over three-dozen Jascha Heifitz transcriptions for Violin and Piano; and less than a month later, with other fall performances of the recital program tucked in between, I would play my very first public performances of the Tchaikovsky Piano Concerto in several Northwest cities—continuing until Thanksgiving.

The solution seemed a matter of saving my strength, resting at every possible opportunity, and organizing my work in such a way that not only would the standards of my performances be where they needed to be, but I should not kill myself in the process. Just days after my last repair surgery in late May, I tackled the big cadenzas at the opening and end of the first movement of the Tchaikovsky, the Scherzando from the middle movement, and the pages of difficult running work toward the end of the third movement. As soon as I got this under my belt, I continued to use the running work as a warm up and conditioning several times throughout the day while practicing each of the two cadenzas and the Scherzando in two or three day rotations, concentrating on just one at a time, until I felt that I'd done as much as I could on each before moving on to the next. With this bunch of material segregated from my study of the piece as a whole so I didn't become discouraged, I tackled the piece as a whole. Learning right off the parts I could learn more quickly, keeping up both momentum and my spirits.

In the meantime, however, there was the matter of the Beethoven Fourth Concerto, which I'd played many times, but which remains a work requiring plenty of practice for which your fingers have to be in top shape. Nevertheless, the Beethoven was an old friend, the first movement of which I would return to daily for the kind of finger work that helps you play everything a little bit better.

In the evenings or at other times when I might be feeling poorly, I could look over the less difficult slow movement and last movement of the Beethoven. As soon as I felt I could put the bulk of the piece aside, a half-dozen passages remained in my daily practice so that speed and endurance in these most difficult bits would not be an issue when I returned to the whole concerto later in the summer. At one point, just before I began my radiation on July 1st, I took several days and just practiced the cadenzas until I was totally satisfied. I would not be able to return to most of this piece until two months later, only a couple of weeks before my performance, well along in the toxic radiation process, and did not know what condition I would be in at that point.

Beginning in mid-May, every afternoon I worked on the transcriptions for my recording, with Sherry starting with the very hardest—and they were tough. Because, while at Eastman, I had done some study with Brook Smith, the pianist who partnered with the legendary Heifitz for many years,—and also because Sherry was a student and the assistant to Heifitz himself (who bequeathed to her the Tononi violin on which she would record), I felt a special responsibility about my role in this recording. My work had to reflect taking a leap of faith and looking way beyond any acceptable standards to the very limits of my imaginative and musical abilities. Beyond my immediate concerns as the pianist in the duo, I learned the violin part carefully. In examining every detail of Heifitz's meticulous markings for the piano, I employed every trick of balance, coloring, rubato, and general finesse I could muster.

Toward the first of August as I finished my radiation treatments, the recital program with the tough Chausson was pretty much 'in my fingers,' and I would begin to pull together the Beethoven Concerto for the mid-month performance. My work on the Heifitz transcriptions had been so good that in the weeks approaching the mid-August recording sessions I had no difficulty in making them ready.

The stickler was the Tchaikovsky. I just didn't seem to have the physical energy to feel comfortable with this athletic piece. I limited my practice to lots of very light playing, so that in my physical condition, and my anxiety over strength or endurance, I didn't compound the problem by adding stiffness and habits of forcing to the formula. A month later, when the Beethoven and Chausson performances, as well as the recording sessions, were behind me, suddenly my view of the Tchaikovsky changed. Perhaps just by virtue of having less on my plate with which to deal, the practice actually started feeling good. I could dig in and find my muscles beginning to work again.

Many people during that time were deeply concerned about me. Although I cannot say that all my playing represented my very best, some was darned good, and nothing below an acceptable level. The lesson I tried to follow was of knowing one's limits and not allowing fear and anxiety to rule the day. Under any circumstances, should you wake up the day of a performance and find yourself sick in bed, stay in bed. Don't force yourself up and use the energy you should be saving for the stage, trying to see if your wings still work. Remember the golden rule of all performing, especially under less than good circumstances: play on the interest, not the principal of your abilities.

Closing

Although perhaps not the main subject of this little book, my cancer battle was without doubt the lens through which all has been viewed and remembered. Tough as it was, surviving the tremendous difficulty of those years not only made me a better person, but also provided a clear demonstration of the true value of my relationship to the art of music and piano playing.

During that medical ordeal and the additional personal losses that followed in its wake, music provided a special kind of personal lifeline, resilient and strong. I clung to the centuries of genius, of love, of worship entwined in its fiber by the great composers and the high priests of the art of playing the piano. My instinctive faith in its value would ultimately serve to pull me safely through terror and loss, reaffirming my innate love of life as I clung.

This musical lifeline was perhaps an improbable but very real personal faith lurking within me; one long ago cast in my direction perhaps by God Himself, with the knowledge that to it I would instinctively cling. It may very well have been His hand itself, for as I would tighten my grip, with fear and hope, bracing myself against yet unknown rigors, this thing seemed almost to grip back, pulling me just a little bit surer toward eventual reprieve. At times I could almost hear, "Hang on, this too will pass"—words of comfort spoken to me during difficult times in my childhood by my mother, now spoken by a larger voice. During the hardship I was learning the true value of my years of hands-on worship of something in life greater and more lasting than myself.

Clinging to my work, by the light of its wonder, I lived day by day, minute by minute, second by difficult second according to the living examples of the great teachers I had known in my life whose own lives demonstrated living by uniting earthly life with the spiritual reckonings of their actions and attitudes. The bleak reality of what my life had become and would remain for over a decade became, simply by its full acceptance, in light of their example and bolstered by my daily practice, not only tolerable but even a badge of honor. With difficulty as the daily norm, I reaffirmed my love of life by a daily task of planning just one activity of pure pleasure or enjoyment for myself. From a half hour to a half a day, not the activity itself nor the length of time in its pursuit, but the exercise in its choice and planning provided the biggest dividend. Despite all I endured, I was still able to enjoy life.

I began de-junking my life, first with my closets, giving or throwing away any article of clothing I did not or could not wear. Then the process continued by replacing a personal phone book the size of the Manhattan directory with a pocket-sized volume. I was reevaluating everything and every person in my life. In the process, left with less, I quickly felt just how in love with life, even with the scant remains of my life, I truly was.

As I plodded from surgery to surgery, I began to just ignore looking into mirrors, choosing instead to see myself reflected in the eyes or voices of those whom I valued. I discovered that the reality of my face was only a small part of my self-image. As a once handsome face became first scarred and then corrupted past any complete return, I carried within another version of myself like that in a small locket. This was not what some people saw, but to my surprise, others with clearer eyes seemed to perceive the man in that locket, the man living on, growing, full of life to yet live, full to overflowing with love of life, of others and of the things dear to him.

This last blessing, however, was also the source of some of my most troubling moments. To be a long-term patient is to be in a kind of prison. I was not fully aware of the degree of that confinement until I approached the general end of the ordeal and began to look back. Over the many years and surgeries my basic love of life seemed never to have taken a time off nor to have retreated politely to a posture befitting a soul under siege. Instead, it seemed to burst forward, illuminating all I saw in radiant light—the casual scent of a flower was now a beguiling perfume, good food became darned near an X-rated experience, a major roller coaster (or in the case of a memorable day of two-dozen whoppers at

LA's Magic Mountain amusement park) a near reason for living.

I may not have liked what my life had become, but I was still very much in love with life in general. My continuing musical efforts and renewed interests in long-neglected hobbies and diversions helped me to understand this crucial difference. I believe this dichotomy was both the key to my survival as well as the source of some difficulties. In this tumultuous state I found clearer meaning in a remembered piece of haiku poetry which summed up the positive side of the conundrum. Loosely translated:

> ***That I exist***
> ***is a perpetual surprise***
> ***which is life.***

At the same time, in the fight of my life, although prevailing, I was paying dearly for doing so. The truth of losing a career and the life toward which I had worked since my youth was also beginning to sink in. So, too, did my friends scattered around the country seem steadily to lose both artistic and personal interest in me. As the years of living in the medical trenches had ground on, and the bulk of my playing was suspended, the true frailty of a social life bound up with my career began to be revealed.

I had heard about movie and television stars gradually dropped by friends and the members of their profession due to protracted illnesses. A poignant interview with Burt Reynolds came to mind during which he described this in his own life. My first efforts to maintain ties had most often received reactions of great concern, but shortly the natural ease of long-forged relationships began to deteriorate as I found myself upstaged by my medical dilemma. It was as if the reality of my life had become either inconvenient or uncomfortable to those whom I had considered friends. I was dropped.

I began to see the musical world continuing fully on without me. Perhaps most painful was the occasional accidental hearing of one of my own performances on the radio. Valued professional relationships began to strain, for as I was fighting for my life and doing all I could to maintain my playing, and at least a tentative connection with a musical career, inevitable reports of my lack of important activity also drifted in. I actually received and kept a letter from Steinway, not only suspicious in tone but containing ridiculous accusations over my loyalties—genuinely insulting and more hurtful than could be imagined. I began behaving as one pulling the covers over his head.

In this state, with my growing love of life contrasted with the loss of my life's work and an increasing feeling of isolation from others, my understanding from many performances of Liszt's colossal tone poem for the piano, Vallée d'Obermann, began to take on new meaning. Liszt's work is a musical response to Lord Byron's passionate outpouring of a man entangled in a similar dilemma:

> Could I embody and unbosom now
> That which is most within me, could I wreak
> My thoughts upon expression, and thus throw
> Soul, heart, mind, passions, feelings, strong or weak
> All that I would have sought and all I seek,
> Bear, know, feel, and yet breathe, into one word,
> And that one word were lightning, I would speak.
> But as it is, I live and die unheard,

With a most voiceless thought, sheathing it as a sword.

On one hand, the combined results of my protracted battle had set me strangely apart from others, feeling stranded and even afraid. Yet sometimes I nearly felt like stopping a passerby to talk about life's overwhelming sweetness. However, any imagined response would be only polite at best, problematic at worst. I was splitting in two—my basic optimism at war with inevitable professional bad news and increasing social isolation. I stopped answering the phone, opening mail and even going out to the store to buy food.

My playing had remained the absolute exception from this turmoil, but eventually it too began to succumb to the confusion which had become my life. In my infrequent public performances, as I started experiencing serious memory lapses, a problem from which I had never suffered, I was compelled to set aside even these efforts.

Whether this dilemma was preventable or inevitable I do not know, but it was difficult and would take time and working through the descent into a first-class personal depression before subsiding. During this difficult period I wrote the bulk of this book, and by doing so, looking warmly at the fortunate events of my past, began to find my way forward. In the middle of the writing process itself another part of the equation to my survival came into view: the nature and meaning of personal loss.

Since my childhood, due to my conspicuous talent, wonderful teaching, and hard work, I had the good fortune of support and enthusiastic encouragement all around. Even the reluctance of my athletically inclined father faded during my teenage years, making him my number one fan. I don't think a single student of his many classes at Portland State University failed to hear about his son's playing and competition victories.

As a result of all this adulation and the pressure, applied both from within as well as inferred by the support of others, I became and remained very much at the center of my own concerns for a very long time. For a concert artist this may be a matter of necessity. In psychological studies, to be a professional concert pianist is to have the occupation ranked as number one most stressful, just over that of brain surgeon. Now in my late forties, having undertaken to have something tangible to show for these years of personal and professional loss, in mid-effort of writing this book I would be fully yanked out of the formative position of general importance in my life, replacing my needs and issues with those of others.

The one lucky exception to the general desert which had become my personal life was my friendship with a fellow who entered my life by helping me with the building of my studio. During this time, as I went in and out of surgery, Terry provided a special kind of companionship, finding the time, juggling work and personal responsibilities, for a day of fishing or other shared guy-type activities in the magnificent Oregon wilderness. He helped to reintroduce me to the riches of my life and to the old Mark. In Terry's company I began to feel again whole, strong, happy, and more optimistic. Over the few years of our friendship I grew to value Terry as I might a brother.

On one of our fishing trips Terry drove a hook into his arm and with it, as the worst possible luck would have it, one of the many dangerous bacteria that live in profusion on our skin, but with which our internal workings cannot cope. After several days of increasingly bad flu symptoms worsened until he was nearly unable to walk, in the emergency room, a saga began which would last over a year. With every system of Terry's body including his brain ravaged by an infection that would have killed any less fit person, I became his primary advocate—personally, medically, and even legally. As explained to me by the admitting doctor, the many-sided battle Terry faced would be so complex that he would need the unwavering attention of a round-the-clock advocate. With Terry's poor family situation, the responsibility fell to me, and I undertook it without a second thought.

After two touch-and-go weeks in intensive care, I slept in a chair for the following three months in Terry's hospital room. There I maintained a vigil over every aspect of his chart, making sure that all the details of the doctor's orders were maintained not only by staff but by Terry himself who, a typical former jock, was often less than a cooperative patient. During those months Terry underwent every conceivable horror in a life-and-death struggle that was at times nearly unbearable to watch. Final success even demanded an open-heart surgery to remove the first valve of Terry's heart with a stubborn piece of infecting vegetation.

Two full months in a nursing home followed during which Terry re-emerged from the near-death image of a prison-camp victim to a frail resemblance of his former self. Terry spent the next six months in the basement of our family home, during which I cared for him nearly around the clock, also managing his rehabilitation which included no less than regaining the use of his hands and his ability to walk. Terry lived with the discomfort of blood regurgitating due to the missing first valve in his heart, but would have to wait and become substantially stronger to face a second open-heart surgery for replacement with a prosthetic valve. In the fall, just about one year following the initial accident with the fishing hook, this second arduous surgery took place. In only a few weeks, Terry returned to the stature and vitality that I had once taken for granted.

Alas, Terry's return to good health was all too brief. A few weeks before Christmas, as I was contemplating scheduling my own remaining surgeries, I arrived home one evening to a mass of emergency vehicles in front of the house. Assuming an issue with my aging mother, I rushed to the side door of the house and up the stairs toward her bedroom. To my momentary relief I found her sitting on the edge of her bed, pulling on some clothes as she laughingly described her personal adventure with a young, good-looking fireman coming through the window of her bedroom only moments before. My participation in the laughter was short-lived as I realized that the emergency personnel must be downstairs.

Before I got to Terry's quarters, I was intercepted by a fireman who told me that they were still working on him. He explained that a short while earlier Terry had made a 9-1-1 call, saying that he was a heart patient experiencing extreme arrhythmia. Evidently Terry then tried walking to unlock the side door, making only three or four steps before collapsing dead on the floor.

Over the next months I dreaded going to sleep due to tormenting dreams with Terry's persistent visits. These were not dreams in the normal sense. It seemed as if Terry was somehow visiting me in my dreams, expressing unwillingness to go on to the inevitable. With increasingly difficult exchanges, I awoke from one sitting up with tears streaming down my face and Terry's figure still standing at the end of my bed as I insisted he must move on. After the long, difficult battle we'd both fought to its eventual success, the surprise of his death made me feel as if I'd suddenly lost an arm or leg, not able to fully comprehend nor adjust to its absence. However, Terry's frequent dream visits, with his ongoing expressions of guilt and reluctance to leave this life, felt terribly wrong as well. Desperate for some kind of closure, I knew I must do something.

A few days later I went to the family cabin of my old friend Don Robertson, located on the beautiful Metolius River in Central Oregon. I hoped that, alone in this lovely setting, one in which I felt safe and happy, I could find some peace from the torment of Terry's sudden passing. After a good first night's sleep, I awoke with the sun, set a fire in the heavy iron stove so to heat the cabin, and returned to bed.

Terry had always carried a lovely old Dunhill lighter, which he had received as a gift. As I drifted back to sleep, I dreamt I was in the safety of an attic bedroom—the kind of cozy upstairs bedroom usually inhabited by a boy. As I glanced down to a small table, there was Terry's gold lighter. Upon noticing it, suddenly there were two, then three, then four and five, and I knew that Terry was coming to visit once again. I also knew, however, that this visit would be different, feeling somehow that it had been arranged.

I glanced across the room to the top of a staircase and sure enough he appeared, dressed in his habitual clean Levis and a white T-shirt, but this time, in a beautiful full-length, dark-blue, cashmere overcoat as well. It now seemed clear what was happening. I noticed that despite a warm smile on his face, his green eyes were still half-closed as they had been in death on the basement floor. We said our goodbyes, wishing each other well, and that we would, along with all the people in life that we had loved, be together someday again. With that we embraced, and I woke up with a smile on my face, jumped out of bed laughing, and ran out into the warm summer air, grateful to know that Terry was on his way. I carry the gold Dunhill lighter with me everywhere.

With Terry's passing I was beginning to learn new lessons about the nature and meaning of loss. Despite losing so much in my own life I began to find a certain acceptance in doing so, as if loss and love are simply two sides of the same coin. To reach out for one is by necessity to accept the inevitability of the other. If one does not love, one is safe from feeling loss. But on the other hand, if one dares to love, then loss needs to be faced honestly and accepted as a healthy and inevitable price of loving— neither hated nor feared but graciously understood and quietly paid.

Through his friendship and all we enjoyed together, Terry helped me to overcome an all-consuming anger. As I looked back on my role in Terry's own struggle, despite the tragedy of his death, I had no regrets. As I continued writing and looking back over the history of my life, thanks in large part to Terry, despite all the loss of recent years, I also had no regrets.

The passing of two others dear to me showed me new ways to view the inevitable loss we must all face in life. After several minor strokes during her eighties, just prior to her ninetieth birthday, my mother experienced a big stroke that sent her into medical care for the remaining months of her life. On what proved to be her last day, I stopped by the nurses' station to chat about a bit of minor lung congestion being treated. Expecting nothing unusual, I entered her room to find her sitting stiffly upright in her bed, terrified and gasping for air with a horrible guttural sound, as if she were drowning in her own fluids.

Throwing my arms around her, I told her I loved her and that I'd be right back with the doctor if she could hold on for just a few seconds. I bolted into the hallway to see the nurse already calling the doctor and signaling that she would be on her way in seconds. Terrified and in a near panic, instead of running back to the room, with the nurse on the way I ran down the hall, dropping to my knees just behind the men's room door, and began to pray frantically. "God, take her. Please take her now! This is too much. I'll go crazy if she has to go through this. Please take her now—and if you can't, please help me to endure this, because I think I'll go crazy."

I got to my feet, threw open the door and took a lunging first stride just as the nurse appeared at her door with her hands held in the air, "It's all right. She's gone."

As I slowed to a walk, I called back, "Thank God." And I meant it. When I reached the nurse we embraced, laughing in relief. I went in to say goodbye. When I reemerged the nurse said, "Mark, you were praying, weren't you? That was absolutely miraculous. I've never seen anything like it. The very moment you got behind that door and I entered your mother's room, she just stopped struggling. I tidied her up and combed her hair, and for the first time in some weeks she and I exchanged several sentences. As I held her hand and settled her back against her pillow, she smiled and died."

When losing one's parents, suddenly there is no one between one's self and the grave. My mother's passing helped me to see the eventuality of my own end with a certain peace of mind, along with a compelling suggestion about the power of prayer.

It was my dog Kypp who gave me a master lesson in saying a proper goodbye. Kypp had been my constant companion during all the surgeries, helping me to feel safe, loved, and just glad to be home and alive. Whether Kypp was my home-duty nurse or my guru is not fully clear.

Like all dogs, Kypp lived utterly in the present, helping me by his loving example to do so as well.

On Kypp's last night he got wearily to his feet and let me know that he needed to go out. This time when I opened the door for him he looked over his shoulder until I understood that he wanted me to follow him outside. We filed slowly out to the front yard and into the warm night air. He sat and looked again my way until I got the idea and sat down beside him. A light silky breeze moved through the birch trees illuminated by an ivory moon. As we sat together listening to the swish of the wind moving through a million small leaves, Kypp placed his paw on my leg and looked up at me. I bent down, cradling him close to me. As he kissed me tenderly on the cheek, I saw every moment of our life together and felt fortunate to have had such a friend.

The next night I took him to a twenty-four hour vet. As I held him in my arms and smiled affectionately, he looked trustingly back and slipped away. His grace and sweetness in facing the death he knew was coming showed me that only the good is worth considering at life's end.

With the long hours of lonely practice, the strict personal discipline and sacrifice, a young, aspiring pianist discovers he is devoted to a jealous and demanding mistress. Difficult to keep straight in one's mind, with the reality of those demands on one hand and the expectation and prejudices of the members of the professional musical world on the other, is that the road toward true artistry is not that of becoming what one is not, but to search for and distill that which one in fact is. That endeavor can be the loneliest one imaginable. Aside from the practice of heeding my own counsel, young as I was, my persistent study and practice kept me from going astray during a time in which the events of my life seemed to make about as much sense as Alice in Wonderland.

Despite its complexity and a labyrinth of problems large and small, good piano playing and good music making in general are finally matters of basic earnestness, combined with the simple joy of sharing something one loves and cherishes. Perhaps the most challenging part of becoming a successful performer is hearing one's playing as others do. The development of one's artistic identity is a strange and seemingly incompatible mixture of self-acceptance on the one hand, while learning at the same time to deny or transcend oneself in favor of the music—perhaps like stepping out of one's own way. This process is a daily exercise in enlarging both one's confidence and single-mindedness, while at the same time embracing a kind of humility and level of self-scrutiny beyond the understanding of most people. Great playing exists only in the moment, eluding all static measures, descriptions, or attempts to codify or otherwise nail down any process in its pursuit. It's like the hunch of an idea that feels as if it's just around the next corner, or perhaps an itch that seems to move endlessly around, evading just one good scratch.

During my mid twenties, my efforts toward a career seemed chaotic—like a juggling act during which an extra ball seemed constantly to be at hand. Throughout this period of leap-frog optimism and disappointment, two opposites seemed in constant partnership: the highs or the good times that came along seemed to happen at a time when virtually no one was around with whom to share an all too short-lived moment of joy; so often however, when I was all but at the brink of despair, some unsolicited kindness of a total stranger found its way to my life, perhaps due to the image of a young man reaching for something just beyond his grasp. These kindnesses, too many to retell, made it possible to continue on what would remain a chaotic but happy journey.

During these years, it may have been a mistake on my part not to have had more contact with other young and aspiring artists, particularly pianists. I believe this was a result of being a bit shy socially as well as a bit stubborn in finding my own way. However, this lonely path may have actually been the source of some of the genuinely individual characteristics which would develop in my playing. Perhaps the void that surrounded me created a necessity in which I had to find for myself, on my own terms, regardless of a line of the very finest teachers one could imagine in whose shadow I existed, my own style—my own way to the heart of the musical matter.

These were tough times. Yet they were some of the most wonderful of my life. I learned that the true measure of anything in this life is weighed in terms not of what it can bring, but by the awareness of that which one is willing to sacrifice in order to pursue it. While succeeding, per sé, seemed often to evade me, somehow the simple joy of my personal pursuit of the music itself, along with the delight of sharing it with others sustained me, drove me on, and gave me faith.

Years later, with the experience of a teacher at all levels from beginners to grad students at university, I have come to believe that to impart to our children a zeal for the pursuit of excellence is not only the key to personal development, but may be at the heart of our social health as a nation. Any such motivated pursuit is, in my way of thinking, a 'hands on' act of worship. The trick for those of us who teach, or who are parents or some other form of authority figure, is to be careful not to equate any endeavor on the basis of that with which we ourselves are familiar, interested, or assume to be of universal value. What's important is simply the pursuit of excellence, regardless of where it is directed. The value of this, the life lessons, and the self-esteem which is forged comes from the efforts themselves. Any moments of 'success' or 'failure,' although they can make moments flicker brilliantly or sting poignantly, are strictly momentary in the long run. Such goals are important to some people as steps are to climbing upward. But they are all transcended by the long-term and inevitable sense of personal meaning—a sense of self, keenly and vibrantly tied by one's own efforts to the life around. In my opinion, the pursuit of excellence is the indispensable element of discovering one's self as well as a sense of meaning relative to life. Strive for excellence. Discover meaning. Find happiness.

I am grateful beyond words to the encouragement of my friends in writing this book. Nearly all was written toward the end of a decade-long battle with a very stubborn cancer during which only sporadic visits onstage to play for the public were possible. For about a decade and a half before this ordeal, I had finally realized my dream and was playing many concerts all over the world. I suppose it could be said that I have lost, or perhaps set aside, more in terms of career and professional goals and personal security than most people even dream of having. But such measurements, although valid in the eyes of a friend or family member, seem to me an embarrassment or at least utterly inappropriate as I reflect on the privilege and simple joy of the opportunity I had as a youngster and young man to pursue with all my heart and all my strength something in this life I dearly love. The bounty from this quest, revisited and renewed in this telling, has been the source of my faith and survival.

As I have remembered back on these and many other stories, some of which with a pang of guilt I must admit to wishing I had included here, it has struck me how difficult it has been to clearly recall the great disappointments. And believe me there were great disappointments—and many of them. As a matter of fact, it's possible that for most artists of any kind in this world, disappointment might be the norm of nearly every day. Over and over while I have so little at this moment in tangible order to show for the many years of labor and love, how is it that I have looked back with a feeling of such good fortune? It seems to me that my understanding of the problem one faces of separating the good from the bad of one's life went back to my childhood and the simple joy I felt for music and other life wonders which caught my eye or ear or heart. The great and rare gift that I received was only that of the opportunity to follow my heart and the quiet wisdom of parents who helped me at an early age to understand the value of pursuing excellence.

The greatest treasure in life is simply the chance to connect with something better and more lasting than oneself. While most folks wander through their life not even aware that such things exist, only the lucky few learn that such treasures cannot be bought or seized by virtue of position or power, but obtained only by great and enduring personal commitment and effort. Even fewer have the chance to hold such beauties in their hands and, as they shape that which they love, so shape their lives and themselves.

Like the monk discarding worldly excesses, one's vision gets clearer as one's needs get simpler. Sacrifice starts to look like a simple matter of choosing, and by abandoning that which must be left behind, one finds not only one's true self, but a surprising spiritual treasure within—infinitely richer and more enduring than even the fruits of the Herculean efforts garnished in pursuit of the task.

One's work is sacred.